T-6

A PICTORIAL RECORD OF THE HARVARD, TEXAN AND WIRRAWAY

Books by Peter C. Smith

DESTROYER LEADER
TASK FORCE 57
(Foreword by Admiral of the Fleet, Lord Fraser of North Cape)
PEDESTAL
(Foreword by Admiral of the Fleet, The Lord Lewin)
STUKA AT WAR
(Foreword by Oberst Hans-Ulrich Rudel)
HARD LYING
BRITISH BATTLE CRUISERS
WAR IN THE AEGEAN
THE STORY OF THE TORPEDO BOMBER
HERITAGE OF THE SEA
ROYAL NAVY SHIPS' BADGES
R.A.F. SQUADRON BADGES
BATTLES OF THE MALTA STRIKING FORCES
PER MARE, PER TERRAM
(Foreword by The Earl Mountbatten of Burma)
FIGHTING FLOTILLA
(Foreword by Mrs R.M.J. Hutton)
ARCTIC VICTORY
DESTROYER ACTION
(Foreword by Admiral Sir Gresham Nicholson)
BATTLE OF MIDWAY
THE GREAT SHIPS PASS
HIT FIRST, HIT HARD
(Foreword by Vice-Admiral B.C.B. Brooke)
IMPACT!
ACTION IMMINENT
CRUISERS IN ACTION
DIVE BOMBER!
HOLD THE NARROW SEA
H.M.S. WILD SWAN
(Foreword by Bob Burns)
INTO THE ASSAULT
VENGEANCE!
JUNGLE DIVE BOMBERS AT WAR
VICTORIA'S VICTORIES
(Foreword by David Chandler)
THE ROYAL MARINES – A PICTORIAL HISTORY
(Foreword by Lieutenant-General Sir Steuart Pringle)
MASSACRE AT TOBRUK
DIVE BOMBERS IN ACTION
BATTLESHIP ROYAL SOVEREIGN
EAGLE'S WAR
STUKA SQUADRON

For Arthur and Audrey Pearcy

Good friends indeed in hour's need!

T-6

A PICTORIAL RECORD OF THE HARVARD, TEXAN AND WIRRAWAY

PETER C. SMITH

Motorbooks International
Publishers & Wholesalers

This edition first published in 1995 by Motorbooks International,
Publishers & Wholesalers, PO Box 2, 729 Prospect Avenue,
Osceola, WI 54020, USA.

Previously published by Airlife Publishing Ltd, Shrewsbury, England, 1995

Library of Congress Cataloging-in-Publication Data is available

ISBN 0-7603–0191–3

Printed and bound in Singapore.

Contents

Preface

Acknowledgements 9

1 Origins and Ancestors 11

2 The SNJ/T-6 Development 27

3 The Versatile Harvard 47

4 The Wirraway Story 69

5 Exports and Offspins 83

6 A Re-Birth and Re-Generation 101

7 At War 125

8 At Work and at Play 143

Appendix 1: T-6 Namecheck 155

Appendix 2: T-6 Variant Listing 156

Preface

The T-6 and its many variants have had a lifespan of more than fifty years so far. During that time it has served with almost every air force in the world in a wide variety of roles. Since its demise as a front-line military training aircraft its versatility has ensured equal global coverage in hands of the display team and the enthusiast as well as the aeronautical museum.

This book has attempted to cover pictorially the many facets of this hugely versatile and uniquely ubiquitous aircrafts' repertoire as is possible within a limited number of pages. While it is obvious that not every aspect of the T-6's career could be encompassed, effort has been made to include a broad range of subjects.

In my search for photographs I have contacted air forces, museums, flying teams, individual owners, enthusiasts and first-rate aerial photographers the world over. Not all my searches were successful. Many air forces, including, sadly, the Royal Air Force, could not see their way to helping. Many others ignored all requests and the same situation was found from other individuals and organisations who had splendid material but were not willing to make it available. This is a sad reflection of modern attitudes but, happily, this type of reaction was far outweighed and indeed was swamped by the generous and willing support and the enthusiastic backing of others from all parts of the world, eager to share their best and their love of the T-6 with a wider audience.

I do not claim to have uncovered a startling amount of fresh information, although this volume does contain much that has not been included between hard covers before. A few myths have been laid; for example – gallant and dramatic as the use of the Mosquitoes was during the Korean War, it is NOT the case, as is frequently claimed, that this represented the *first* military use of such machines in this role. The work of the LT-6Gs was as brave and stirring an episode of the T-6's life as any, but it was *preceded* by identical work conducted by the Australian Wirraways between 1943 and 1945, and by equally effective action by Harvards of the Royal Indian Air Force during the 1947 Kashmir conflict. Nor have I found the slightest documentary evidence to support the oft-trumpeted claim that a German submarine was sunk by a Mexican T-6 during the World War II. However, as a historian of long standing, I stand prepared to eat my words at any time!

As for my own errors, I am sure to have made some in a book of this nature. I apologise for these in advance and will hope to make corrections (and perhaps additions) in future editions of the book. I have tried to update material as far as possible to include interesting stories up to the end of 1989, as well as a balanced historic perspective. Inevitably of course, not everyone's favourite T-6 topic, aircraft or story will be included here, but I trust that my selection is as comprehensive as it could possibly be made.

In view of the valuable combat work done by ground-to-air rocket attacks post-war in Korea by American T-6s, it was natural that similar experimentation should take place elsewhere with standard rockets mounted on rails beneath the wings, and that the Harvard should be so adapted that training in this form of attack could be part-and-parcel of its itinerary.

The North American in fact proved a good steady platform for the delivery of such ordnance against land targets and its low speed made for accurate targeting. Here Harvard 2930 of the Royal Canadian Air Force carries out such shooting with three rockets fired and a fourth yet to leave the rack. Notice also the four small practice bombs in place outboard of the rocket mountings on each of the aircraft's wings. The chequered tail markings are typical of RAF and RCAF squadrons during the 1950s period when this photograph was taken, although the exact date is not known. (*Courtesy of Canadian Forces Photographic Unit, Ontario*)

Acknowledgements

From the vast amount of really superb photographic material made available it has been a very difficult task to trawl down to the section presented here. The parameters which decided the final selection were guided by the following factors, each of which had to be balanced carefully. There was the need for as complete an historical coverage as possible and as universal a coverage as possible. These requirements did not always sit happily for the over-riding concern of both author and publisher alike for *quality* of photograph. Finding fifty-year-old photographs to illustrate rare and special windows on the T-6's long career while attempting to couple that with the very high standards demanded by the printing and photographic requirements of the 1990s caused the author many a headache. As always in such cases, compromise has to be made. So, if a particular use or incident is not pictured in these pages it is more likely that the quality of the original negative brought about its omission rather than lack of such a photograph in the first place. We hope the reader will understand the dilemma and accept that the aim of presenting as high a quality of reproduction as possible was done with their interests in mind.

So many otherwise deserving or unique photographs I had to leave out. But I would like to thank the following individuals and organisations, presented here in strictly alphabetical order, for their highly-appreciated contributions and help, whether used or not, all of which helped make this book as careful and appreciative a tribute to the T-6 family as possible. For those who gave permission for their outstanding pictorial work to be reproduced in this book, a very special thank you.

William J. Armstrong, Department of the Navy, Washington, DC; Colonel Sabri Aydogan, Ministry of Defence, Ankara; D.S. Baker, Hawker de Havilland Victoria Ltd, Melbourne; Dr Fred Beck, Office of Air Force History, Bolling AFB; Major-General Ahmed I. Behery, Commander Royal Saudi Air Force, Riyad; Mrs Anne Bell, Fleet Air Arm Museum, Yeovilton; M. Benoits, SIRPA, Paris: David V.S. Berrington, Ohai; Warrant Officer P.L. Boulton, Air Staff Defence HQ, Wellington; Chaz Bowyer, Mulbarton; Commander B.J. Bromfield, Royal Australian Navy, RAN Air Station Nowara; Jack Bryant, TAGS, Langley; Meg Campbell, Palmerston North; Herr Cimander, Armando da Silva Coelho, Forca Aerea Portuguesa, Lisbon; Der Bundesminister der Verteidigung, Bonn; Group Captain B. Cole, Ghanian Air Force HQ, Accra; Dr Ira Chart, Northrop Corporation, Hawthorne, CA; M.B. Chenel, Musée de l'Air et de l'Espace, Le Bourget; John A. Collver, Lomita, CA; Terry Dowman, RNZAF Museum, Christchurch; Group Captain Theo J. MacLean de Lange, Rotorua; Chas. Dellow, Mermaid Beach; Steven D. Eisner, Van Nuys, CA; Major K.W. Farrell, Canadian Forces Photographic Unit, Ottawa; Colonel Francesco Fino, Stato Maggiore dell Aeronautuca, Rome; James L.R. Flynn, Ringwood, Vic; Warrant Officer D.W. Gardner, RAAF Museum, Point Cook; Group Captain John E. Gerber, RAAF, Turner, ACT; Wing Commander Arthur Murland Gill, Llanwarne; Colonel H.R. Haberli, Bern; Brian Hall, Myrtle Bank, SA; Anthony E. Hutton, The Squadron, North Weald; Dr J.A.M.M. Janssen, Royal Netherland Air Force, Soesterberg; Coronel Eduardo Jimenez-Carles, Madrid; Lieutenant-Colonel Sidney F. Johnston, Jr, Albuquerque; Lieutenant-Colonel Zeev Lachish, IDF, Tel Aviv; J. Laneiro, Loures; Reine Maily, Canadian Government

Expositions and A.V. Centre, Ottawa; Doug McPhail, Dundas, Ontario; Cyril J.B. MacPherson, East Ringwood, Vic; Ten QFO Solandge Teixeria de Menezes, Ministerio de Aeronautica, Brasilia-DF; Paul L. Muir, Condell Park, NSW; Brigadier-General Hanna Najjar, Royal Jordanian Air Force, Amman; William C. Northrop, Jr, RCMB Inc. Newport Beach; Arthur Pearcy, Sharnbrook; Bob Piper, Royal Australian Air Force Historical Officer, Canberra ACT; Flight Lieutenant P.B. Ratnayake, Sri Lanka AF HQ, Colombo; Air Commodore S. Sahay, Air HQ IAF, New Delhi; Sadao Seno, Kanagawa-ken; Hanfried Schliephake, Konigsbrunn; F.D. Sheppard, RAF Museum, Hendon; Ray C. Sturtivant, St. Albans; Group Captain Bhisit Sukhum, RTAF, Bangkok; Anna C. Urband; Dept of the Navy, Washington DC; Bill C. Walmsley, Rockwell International, Los Angeles; Nick Williams, American Aviation Historical Society, Waverly, IA; Helen Vaughan-Dawkes, National Archives, Wellington; Nick Veronico, *In Flight*, Woodside, CA; Louis J. Vosloo, Fish Hoek, SA; Dr G.A. 'Doc' Swayze; David Wilson, Department of Defence, Canberra ACT.

Peter C. Smith, Riseley, Bedford.

10

1 Origins and Ancestors

The most widespread and versatile training aircraft ever built; an aeroplane used by more air forces world-wide than any other; a brilliant concept developed and modified through a decade and resulting in more than 17,000 flying machines, more than 600 of which are still flying fifty years later; the best-loved and most-remembered single-engined training aircraft of all time; an adaptable and rugged aircraft that performed in the unexpected roles of fighter aircraft, dive-bomber, COIN airplane, ground-attack machine, observation aircraft, and on extensive anti-guerrilla suppression roles. An aircraft that has served at various times and various dates as airliner, mailplane and pylon racer. The aircraft still most commonly seen at air displays and air races; beloved by stunt aces and formation teams alike but best-remembered as the aircraft that spawned several generations of young pilots in countries as diverse as Brazil and the Soviet Union. All these aircraft are one aircraft, the North American 'T-6'.

The aircraft had almost as many official designations and names as it has uses and users! NA-26, BC-1, NA-44, AT-6, SNJ, 'Texan', J-Bird, Harvard, Wirraway, Ceres and a host more variants, marks and modifications to the same standard design proliferated down the years as engines and concepts changed and were altered around the same basic airframe. And then there were the nicknames bestowed by the flyers themselves down the years 'Pilot Maker', 'Mosquito' and more.

This work is not claimed as *the* definitive history of the T-6, so much as a loving pictorial tribute. The author is continuing exhaustive research for a future major study of the T-6 which is well underway and which will ultimately tell the full and complete story of this, the most universally-utilised and most significant military training aircraft in aviation history. However, for now and in this volume, we must confine ourselves to the salient details and trust our selection of photographs tells the story in its own special way.

The names of North American Aviation and the brilliant designer James H. 'Dutch' Kindelberger, are synonymous. The two first came together when Kindelberger and John Leland 'Lee' L. Atwood, respectively the former vice-president in charge of engineering and chief structural engineer of the Douglas Aircraft Company (both of them active in the development of the equally famed Douglas DC-1 transport aircraft) re-organised the General Aviation Manufacturing Corporation during 1934. The manufacturing operations of this Delaware company, which had originally been founded on 6 December 1928, were taken under the North American name on 1 January 1935. The new base for the re-generated company was the former Curtiss-Caproni factory at Dundalk in Maryland. Meanwhile work commenced on the construction of new plant incorporating the latest assembly techniques and equipment, at the massive Mines Field at Inglewood, California.

Among a host of antecedent operating airline companies and airplane manufacturers that formed the original base of the engineering and manufacturing organization of North American Aviation, were names like Sperry, the Fokker Corporation of America, incorporated in 1923 and acquired by General Aviation in 1930, and the Berliner-Joyce Aircraft Corporation, acquired by North American in the same year and merged in 1933 with General Aviation. By 1938 the new organisation had shed its airline holdings like TWA and concentrated solely on production.

With the outstanding kudos of what was to be the world-famous Dakota design behind them, Kindelberger, Atwood and the team they brought with them, confidently began to enter their advanced concepts for United States Army Air Corps design contracts. The new team scored an instant initial success with their GA-15 observation aircraft, a three-man, mid-wing design, built in less than nine weeks. It won the Air Corps competition at Wright Field, Ohio and became the XO-47 and finally the NA-25, the O-47. Another General Aviation concept, was the GA-16. This was a smaller two-seat in tandem, open-cockpit, low-wing, monoplane training aircraft. Like its contemporaries it was a fabric-covered aircraft, powered by a 400 hp Wright R-975-7 nine-cylinder, air-cooled Whirlwind engine. The GA-16 had been flight-tested under civilian licence number X-2080 at Logan Field, Baltimore and the Air Corps expressed interest. The re-organisation completed, this design was modified and re-introduced for the first time under the North American banner. This was the 'Basic Trainer', which, as the NA-16, Kindelberger entered for the 1934 competition.

As was to be expected, the North American team came up with an aircraft design that incorporated a whole host of radical and innovative features. In effect Kindelberger looked at the Basic Trainer concept laterally and functionally, with one eye on the looming war clouds gathering in Europe and the feel that massive expansion of the world's air forces was imminent and that fighter designs were changing completely with the introduction of monoplane interceptors like the German Me 109, the British Hawker Hurricane and Supermarine Spitfire and the America P-40 on the drawing-boards. Clearly the days of the old 'wings-wires-and-struts' type of biplane trainer were also numbered as a new generation of aircraft would require their pilots to be more highly-skilled in high-speed, low-drag monoplane flying. But it had to be simple enough for novices to fly with some confidence, rugged enough to withstand the treatment handed out by student pilots and versatile enough to be repairable economically. With these widely-differing requirements all firmly in mind the NA-16 was unlike any of its competitors.

First flown by test pilot Eddie Allen on the unauspicious date of 1 April 1935 from Dundalk, the NA-16 had taken six weeks to prepare and by the end of the month was ready to be put through its paces.

The features which won the 1935 Air Corps competition for North American and with it a contract to build forty-two of these training aircraft under the Air Corps designation BT-9, were the same features that ensured this initial order was but the forerunner for seventeen-thousand plus descendants world-wide. They were summarised by the company thus:-

> *(1) Accessibility of internal mechanisms.* By the removal of quickly detachable fuselage side panels and engine cowlings, it was possible to obtain convenient and complete access to the internal structure and mechanisms of the aircraft for inspection, replacements and repairs. This feature was possessed by the BT-9 to a greater extent than by any other aircraft then in existence. It was an extremely important feature to the Air Corps and other purchasers of the aeroplane, concerned then as now with keeping the maximum number of available training aircraft in flying condition.
>
> *(2) Interchangeability of parts and components.* Through design of the airplane in logical components which were quickly detachable and attachable, and through assembly of those components in precision steel jigs, North American achieved a new high in interchangeability. For example, the tips of the wings were designed as quickly detachable assemblies so they could be replaced without a long inactivation period when the wing-tips scraped the runway in a ground loop, as frequently happened when student pilots were at the controls. As another illustration, the entire power-plant installation was designed as a unit, which could be detached and replaced in a matter of eight man hours. Or, an entire wing outer panel could be removed with amazing

speed because it was held to the centre section simply by bolts through flange angles.

(3) Duplication of handling characteristics of combat aircraft. To a remarkable degree, the BT-9 and its descendants duplicated the performance characteristics of single-engined combat aircraft. The transition from a trainer airplane to a pursuit or attack airplane was thus made easier for the student pilot, and the Air Corps training programme was greatly facilitated.

The BT-9 itself was modified by Air Corps requirements to feature an enclosed aerodynamic canopy over the whole of the considerably-widened tandem cockpit and the instruments changed to suit the laid-down Army-style layout. Otherwise the airplane was much the same, other than for an enlarged air intake for the Whirlwind engine forward of the cockpit. Perhaps the most retrograde feature in an otherwise very forward-looking design was the fixed-undercarriage with each fully-faired oleo leg mounted on the forward edge of the central wing section. The wheels themselves were spatted outboard only. The initial use of fixed-landing gear on the NA-16 may have been for strength.

The fuselage was a fabric-covering over a steel frame, and the three-piece wings were all-metal, stressed-skin and flush riveted, all features common to the DC-2, with the two outer panels bolting to a constant-chord centre-section. The wings were forty-two feet in length with a full-span flap on the wing centre section balanced by split flaps on both outer wing panels. These outer panels, leading and trailing edges, as well as the wing dihedral angle, also matched that of the DC-2. As related above, the fuselage was constructed in sub-assemblies for easy replacement, with the separate sections of the engine cavity, cockpit area, upper and lower rear fuselages all being bolted together and fitted with fabric-covered easy-access panels to allow engineers to reach any section of the fuselage simply and quickly.

The basic Army paint scheme of the period was for a blue fuselage with yellow wings and the resultant prototype machines received the company designation of the NA-18. Further modifications, for which provision was made at that time, was for the replacement of the Whirlwind with a 600 hp Pratt & Whitney R-1340 Wasp power-plant and the mounting of machine-guns for armament training. It was proposed that two fixed forward-firing .30 calibre weapons be fitted to the cowling with a single gun of the same calibre on a flexible mounting in the rear cockpit. But the Army rejected both concepts. But of course North American had other fish to fry when it made these provisions, for the Air Corps were far from their only potential customers as we have seen. Nor was it being marketed abroad solely as a trainer.

The first production BT-9 flew on 15 April 1936. In the event, the second Air Corps production order was for forty more aircraft. BT-9As (NA-19s) were equipped with modified outer wing panels to overcome an initial stall problem, which featured a two degree 'wash-out' built into them. Stability was also improved by lengthening the fuselage by five inches overall and the aircraft had built-in provision for both machine-guns and cameras. The fitting of leading edge slats to the outer wing sections necessitated the relocation of the Pitot tube inboard, which gave a long-range clue between the two models. A solitary fixed forward-firing .30 gun was provided on the starboard side of the cowling with a single flexible-mounted weapon of the same calibre in the aft cockpit. The height of the canopy had been increased slightly for crew comfort.

These minor alterations completed, the BT-9 proved a great success in service, so much so that, in 1937 the Air Corps came back with repeat orders for no less than 117 aircraft. The following year the Army dropped the machine-gun requirement once again and as the BT-9C sixty-seven further machines were ordered for use by the USAAC Organized Reserve. Only one BT-9D was ever built. This was an experimental aircraft which appeared in 1938 and was a BT-9B with the tail surfaces and wing panels re-designed for trials.

It was to meet the requirements of the other major Stateside customer, the United States

Navy, that the soundness of the alternative engine design thought out earlier came to the fore. The US Navy did not rate the Wright engine very highly and had always favoured the Pratt & Whitney instead. To meet that preference, and so open up the BT-9 to Navy orders, North American took the first standard BT-9C and replaced the Wright engine with a 600 hp Pratt & Whitney R-1340-41 Wasp radial. Because of dire shortage of funds the Navy was unable to finance this experiment, so this aircraft, the NA-28, became the Army Y1BT-10. This was later redesignated as the BT-10. Evaluation testing followed.

Meanwhile the US Navy had approved the Pratt & Whitney-engined BT-10 and when they had sufficient funds, under the 1937 naval estimates, they immediately ordered forty of these aircraft under the designation NJ-1. Under Navy nomenclure N stood for training aircraft, J for the North American company and 1 indicted the first machine from this firm. All these NJ-1s featured the relocation of the engine airscoop from the top of the cowling to below it. None of the naval trainers were equipped with any armaments. Nor were they equipped for carrier deck landings and none had tail hooks or strengthening.

Deliveries commenced as early as July 1937. The US Navy colour scheme at that time was bright aluminum fuselage and wings with the upper-wing surfaces a vivid orange. Those aircraft utilised for instrument training were distinguished by broad red bands around both fuselage and wings.

All these machines were to be fitted with the Wasp engine except for the final production model of the series. This machine was fitted with yet another alternate power-plant, the 550 hp Ranger XV-770-4 inline engine. This gave a whole new profile to the BT-9 (or the NJ-2 as this aircraft was for a while designated), but the experiment was not a happy one and, after reversion to the normal power-plant, this aircraft was finally delivered to the Navy as a standard NJ-1.

The fitting of the Pratt & Whitney engine with its greater power to the Navy variants, gave a strong performance to the basic model and led to the next home-orientated development. By fitting the 450 hp Pratt & Whitney R-985-25 Wasp Junior engine to the new BT-9D (NA-58) another great stride forward was made.

The NA-58 saw the composite fabric-covered fuselage dropped in favour of the more revolutionary all-metal, aluminium semi-monocoque type of construction, which was both sturdier and lighter. The fuselage was lengthened by fourteen inches. By contrast the wing span was reduced to forty-one feet, by having a broad-chord, but squared-off, wing-tip following further stability tests. The forward edge of the vertical tail surface was much further raked and the formerly distinctly rounded rudder was cut in a sharply angular style that was to become one of the aircraft's most highly distinctive recognition points. Other physical feature changes were brought about by the need for a larger cowling for the new engine, with the exhaust-pipe positioned astern of it on the starboard side. Taking on a decisively modern appearance, the YBT-14's undercarriage still stubbornly remained of the fixed, half-spatted type as before.

Evaluation by the Army Air Corps proved the advantage of these improvements and with re-armament at last gaining some momentum in the States as a result of the international situation, an unprecedented order for no less than 251 BT-14s was placed. The latter end of this batch, some twenty-seven aircraft, were modified while still under construction in 1941, to carry the 400 hp Pratt & Whitney R-985-11A engine.

In the interim, and with firm US orders safely under their belt as an affirmation to the rest of the world of the soundness of the BT-9 design, production was now well under-way at the new Inglewood plant.

> 'Many export sales were found for the trainer series, each requiring design revisions to the specific requirements of the export customer.'

The first of these customers was France. By the end of 1938 it was clear to the French Government that war with Hitler's Germany was almost inevitable. A purchasing mission, under M. Jean Monnet, was sent to the States to explain their dire needs and see if the

Americans would be willing to help. As Monnet himself stated to Captain John H. Towers of the United States Bureau of Aeronautics, 'The French and British Governments had been compelled to accept the terms of the Munich Agreement solely because of the preponderant strength of the German Air Force . . . both the French and British Governments realized further demands could be expected from Germany.' Due to the lamentable state of their own aircraft industry, France's only hope of building up its air strength quickly lay in the bulk purchase of the latest American types. The stumbling block was the American Neutrality Act. A sympathetic President Franklin D. Roosevelt was trying to have this nullified but had to tread carefully. Delicate negotiations continued apace and finally, on 16 January 1939 M. Monnet's mission sent a cable to Paris recommending that the French Government order 555 aircraft of all types, including fighters, bombers and dive-bombers. But by far the largest part of this intended deal was for 200 North American basic training aircraft. Authorisation was received from Paris to go ahead without further delay.

Supply by the American builders presented no problems, delivery of the aircraft was something else. On 9 November 1939 it was reported that fifty-four North American trainers were crated and ready for shipment to France with five more expected to be ready by the end of that month. The problem for the French was shortage of suitable shipping to transport these machines across the Atlantic in convoy, only three such ships being available for December with a capacity of fifty to sixty aircraft each. German submarine activity also brought about further delay when the ports of destination in mainland France were altered to disembarkation at Casablanca in Morocco. Even when the first aircraft arrived there on Christmas Day 1939, few facilities had been prepared for the disembarkation and assembly of the aircraft.

At the time of the French surrender on 15 June 1940 of the forty North American trainer aircraft received at Casablanca, thirty-eight had been successfully transferred to the French Air Force and the other two were still being assembled.

As the North American NA-57, the French ordered 230 BT-9Bs customised to their own special requirements. These aircraft were therefore fitted with reversed throttles and were powered with the 420 hp Wright R-975-E3 engine. All were delivered (despite the American neutrality laws and other restrictions introduced on the outbreak of war in Europe in September 1939), apart from the final batch of sixteen machines. The French surrender in June 1940 left these aircraft still in the States.

It was thanks to the foresight of M. Jean Monnet himself, who worked hard from 3 September 1939 onwards, that the joint Anglo-French Economic Co-ordinating Commission had been formed to ensure both nations got the best from the United States aircraft industries output during their hour of need.

The British also became beneficiaries of all outstanding French orders for American planes. Thanks to the courage of the French representative on the Anglo-French Purchasing Commission in the United States, all French contracts for American planes and arms were signed over to the British on the night of 17 June 1940.

Thus, as with so many other outstanding aircraft orders for occupied countries, the British Government quickly stepped in and purchased them to prevent them falling into German hands. The sixteen NA-57s were diverted to Canada and taken on the inventory of the Royal Canadian Air Force. Being American training aircraft they were allocated names to fit into the British scheme of things and being training aircraft were named after the famous American college of Yale, these sixteen aircraft becoming the Yale Mark I.

But French orders had not been confined to the NA-57, they had also placed contracts for a further 230 NA-64 trainers, which were Pratt & Whitney-equipped BT-14 aircraft, the R-985-25 type being utilised. Along with all the usual French modifications this later order commenced delivery after the outbreak of the war and was therefore only half complete at the time of the surrender. There were 119 outstanding NA-64s on hand and these were also taken into the RCAF and RAF training schools in Canada, and, confusingly, these were also christened Yale Mk.Is. The reverse throttles and other French fixtures remained unchanged in RCAF service. In a similar manner the many NA-57s and NA-64s that fell into German hands were put to good use by their new owners, the Vichy French Government, who also allowed their use by the Luftwaffe training units in both occupied France and Germany with their *Flugzeugführer Schules* and continued in this use for several years.

Following the US Army requirement for a two-seater trainer issued in 1934, the initial response had come from General Aviation, Dundalk, Maryland. It featured the Wright R-975 400 hp radial engine. When North American took them over this machine received the new designation of NA-16 (X-2080) and first flew in April 1935.

With the introduction of closed cockpits and fairings, streamlining the fixed landing-gear, the NA-16's engine was changed to the Pratt & Whitney R-1340 Wasp. This became the NA-18 for Argentina, but the next batch of forty-two machines ordered by the US Army Air Corps as the NA-19 were given the classification of BT-9. They featured a landing gear that had been moved forward and outer wing slats operated by a manually-operated hydraulic system. The Wasp engine was re-introduced. These were Basic Trainers, but there was a need for an even more tame variant for novice pilots, the Primary Trainer.

The aircraft shown here was in fact the ninth BT-9 ordered from North American by the US Army but was experimentally evaluated in this role as the NA-22 with primary trainer features. This included open cockpits, a Townsend ring cowling and much simplified handling equipment. (*Courtesy of Rockwell International Archives*)

16

The BT-9 itself was modified by Air Corps requirements to feature an enclosed aerodynamic canopy over the whole of the considerably-widened tandem cockpit and the instruments changed to suit the laid-down Army-style layout. There was also an enlarged air intake for the Whirlwind engine forward of the cockpit. The BT-9 proved a great success in service, so much so that, in 1937, the Air Corps came back with repeat orders for no less than 117 aircraft. (*Courtesy of Rockwell International Archives*)

It came about in 1937 that even before the first BT-14 had taken to the sky plans were in hand to convert a standard NA-16 to take the folding landing-gear and this became the North American NA-36. As well as having the aircraft wheels retracting fully into wells in each of the extended wing's main sections, this aircraft was given the acclaimed Pratt & Whitney R-1340-S3H1 air-cooled engine which was rated at 600 hp and drove a twin-bladed variable-pitch propeller.

Although the fuselage at this stage remained fabric-covered, some further re-design work was incorporated which included another canopy modification and the re-introduction of armament fittings. Provision was made for the re-introduction of the single, fixed, forward-firing .30 calibre machine-gun on the starboard cowling and the .30 gun on the flexible mounting aft. The reasons for this were related to Kindelberger's ideas on export potential, but also to demonstrate a new concept he was putting across to enable the Air Force to overcome the limitation of funding on all but pure combat-type aircraft at this period.

The North American concept was that the NA-36 represented not just an advanced trainer but something completely new, as a Basic Combat type of aeroplane. Thus, as the BT-9D (and then as the BC-1) the new trainer was advanced as a kind of cheap, second-level pursuit and attack machine. Such a category was obviously more than just a trainer and thus qualified for more generous funding. When Kindelberger proposed this concept to General Henry H. 'Hap' Arnold, who was to become Commanding General of the Army Air Forces, it won instant approval and a new Army specification was written around the NA-36 for just such a type. Not completely surprisingly in the ensuing competition for such an aircraft, the BC-1 fitted the bill exactly! Thus appeared the NA-26 shown here, or the North American BC-1. (*Courtesy of Rockwell International Archives*)

The NA-44 charge number was allocated on 9 December 1937 to the prototype machine for the Canadian Government (NX-18981). (Factory Serial Number 44-747.) This experimental model was the forerunner of thousands of Harvards supplied by the parent company but also built under licence by the Noorduyn Aviation Ltd., of Montreal, Quebec after the Canadian Government had secured a licence for the manufacture of the type in Canada. The Royal Canadian Air Force received thirty Harvard Mk Is in July, 1939.

The Harvard Mk II entered service on 19 June 1940 and by 1945 a total of 1,876 had been accepted. The first assembly line successor began to appear in April 1941. The Canadian output of this machine reached a total of 2,775 Mk IIs with a peak production rate of 113 per month. Many of the Canadian-built Harvards were delivered to the Royal Air Force, but, even so, the Harvard was the second most numerous aircraft type to serve in the RCAF. The Harvard was 'officially' phased out of the RCAF on 14 December 1960. (*Courtesy of Rockwell International Archives*)

The T-6 was one of the most successful aircraft designs of all times. Its arrival filled an urgently-felt need in the air forces of not just the major powers like the United States, Great Britain, France, Canada and Australia, but a whole host of lesser nations that wished to modernise their air fleets under the impetus of World War II. The Texan was the right aircraft at the right time in more ways than one! But before we examine in detail the enormous diversity of customers for the T-6 and the variety of uses that they put this little aircraft to, let us take a look at the final conventional developments of the type by North American in the closing stages of the war, along with a few of experimental and 'oddball' customisations of the basic airframes that took place during this same period.

Many other nations took the earlier NA types in the pre-Lend-Lease era among them Argentina, Brazil, Chile, China, Honduras, Peru, Sweden and Venezuela all took delivery of such aircraft.

On 30 November 1939, Siam ordered ten of the two-seat NA-69 Attack Bomber variants, equipped with the 785 hp Wright R-1820-F52 Cyclone engine, a three-bladed propeller and five .30 calibre wing-fuselage and swivel-mounted machine-guns and bomb fixtures under the fuselage and wings. They never reached the country of their destination but were appropriated by the USAAC (as the A-27) and expended in defence of the Philippines in 1941-42. Brazil purchased thirty of a similar type (NA-72) and Chile twelve (NA-74). China took delivery of fifteen NA-16-3Cs (NA-48) on 23 February 1938. They were similar to the BC-1 except for the engine.

Concentrating solely on the T-6 variants, Latin-American nations naturally constituted a good market for North American early on. Venezuela ordered three NA-71s (NA-16-3) on 18 January 1940. These aircraft resembled the NA-59 except that they carried two fixed, forward-firing machine-guns. Like the RAF the Venezuelans also omitted the flagpole of a radio mast smack in front of the pilot's vision! Under the designation NA-72 (NA-44, BC-1A) Brazil placed a large order on 13 January 1940 for thirty machines for use as Attack Bombers. They were basically NA-59/AT-6s equipped with two wing-mounted machine-guns and direction-finding (D/F) gear. Finally Chile followed suit on 8 August in the same year with an order for a round dozen NA-74s (NA-44) which were identical to the NA-72, except for the extra provision of under-wing racks for light bombs.

This photo shows one of the first of the export types, one of three NA-45s, the Venezuelan government ordered in 1938. (*Courtesy of Rockwell International Archives*)

(*above*)
The NA-56 was a batch of fifty BT-9Bs which North American constructed for the Government of China from 18 April 1939 onwards. They took the serial numbers 56-1453 to 56-1502. Already fully engaged in a long-running war with Japan, the Chinese were desperate for modern aircraft of all types. It was from export orders like these that the fledgling North American Company kept itself afloat and was able to bring forward its improved designs that were to result in the famous AT-6 later. Already the parenthood is obvious.

At this time, with Hitler gulping down the remnants of Czechoslovakia in Europe as well as the Sino-Japanese situation, the need for training aircraft was beginning to boom all around the world and North American were well placed to benefit from it, even if its own Government were still luke-warm. (*Courtesy of Rockwell International Archives*)

(*below*)
The NA-45 was the North American charge number allocated on 14 December 1937 to three trainers built especially for the Venezuelan Air Force under the designation of NA-16-IGV. The factory serial numbers were 45-693, 45-694 and 45-695. These aircraft had been ordered by Venezuela on 18 January 1940 and resembled the NA-59 (AT-6) except that they carried two fixed, forward-firing machine-guns. Like those built for the Royal Air Force, the Venezuelan aircraft omitted the siting of the massive radio mast right in front of the pilot's vision.

All markings were in Spanish. The national markings were on the rounded rudder (like the BT-9) but the rest of the fuselage was painted jungle green. (*Courtesy of Rockwell International Archives*)

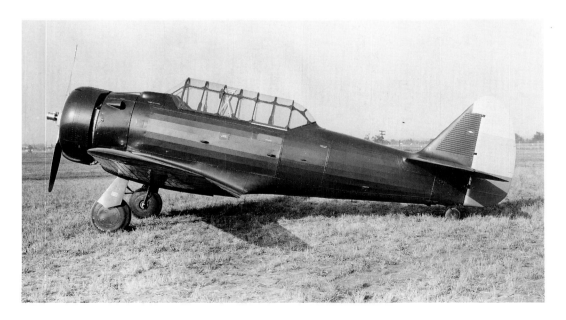

Following the successful completion of the Navy tests an initial batch of sixteen NA-52s was placed, and these joined the fleet in May 1939, under the designation SNJ-1. They were delivered to NAS Anacostia on the 29th of that month in an all-over aluminium finish. It was basically this aircraft that was to interest the British and become the initial Harvard, as we shall see later.

The final transitions now began to take place. A solitary BC-1B was built to test a new centre wing section, increased capacity fuel tanks and an improved version of the retractable landing-gear. All these features would be incorporated on future models.

After the Army had looked hard at its own BC-1s and B-14s and the Navy's SNJ-1s they came up with a new specificiation incorporating the best from each model. Three BC-2s were constructed with the all-metal semi-monocoque, lengthened fuselage and retractable landing gear. The hitherto rounded wing-tips of the BC-1/SNJ-1 duo were squared off in a similar manner to the angular rudder modifications which were also adopted. The air intake became a large and obvious scoop positioned under the forward fuselage behind the cowling. These aircraft also featured an experimental three-bladed propeller fitted to the Pratt & Whitney 600 hp radial R-1340-45 engine which necessitated a second air intake positioned on the port side of the fuselage abaft the cowling. The new propeller was fitted with the hope that this would further improve the aircraft's performance. The experiment took place at Wright Field, Ohio, but was a failure and was not proceeded with. This is the NA-52, or North American SNJ-1 in 1939. (*Courtesy of Rockwell International Archives*)

The North American NA-55, proved itself a winner and the Army placed contracts for fifty-four of these aircraft to equip the Air Reserve training force, with an additional twenty-nine to equip the Air National Guard as the BC-1A. By now the war in Europe was in full-swing, Congress had released enormous funds to increase America's armed forces while they still had the time and the new factories were going flat-out to meet the demand of both home and continued British orders. The need for the Basic Combat designation was seen as no longer applicable, there were ample true Attack types under development as it was. So the category was changed once more to Advance Trainer (AT) and the North American NA-59, as it became, went to war under the designation it was to become most famous, the AT-6. Thus, of the original order for 180 BC-1s the Army had ninety-two modified as BC-1As in which capacity they served mainly as flexible gunnery trainers rather than 'pilot makers'. Nine others stayed in the plant and became the first of the 'AT-6 period' as they were later dubbed by American instructors and trainees alike. Late in 1940 the Army Air Corps placed orders for ninety-four of these AT-6s and the dynasty had commenced.

The North American BC-1A (BC Standing for Basic Combat) became the AT-6 (AT for Advanced Trainer) and combined with all-metal fuselage of the BT-14, slightly lengthened, with the retractable landing-gear and wings which featured the 'squared-off' tips. The rudder became angular in shape and the air intake was made into a shallow scoop positioned slightly abaft the engine cowling. This is a 1941 view which shows some of these features to good advantage. (*National Archives, Washington DC*)

The early war years were studded with problems of supply and delivery for North American due to the political ramifications of neutrality that were not cleared-up until the Lend-Lease Act came into force. 'When a new contract for Harvard trainers was placed with North American late in 1939, the British decided to concentrate training activities in Canada, and to have the Harvards flown directly to training centres in the Dominion. Until revision of the Neutrality Act took effect in September 1940, it was necessary to have these planes pulled across the international boundary by Canadian nationals, where they were turned over to Canadian pilots.

The first plane hauled across the international line by manpower was delivered in the summer of 1940 from Pembina, North Dakota, a small town near the Canadian border. Altogether about twenty-five Harvards were delivered in this fashion before direct delivery was legalized. Subsequently the Harvards were flown direct from the factory near Los Angeles to the training bases where they would be used in Canada. This tremendous delivery job was performed by a staff of skilled American pilots who delivered the trim monoplanes in Canada and returned by scheduled airlines for the next delivery flight. By the end of 1940 North American had delivered more than 800 Harvard advanced trainers to various parts of the British Empire. In January 1941 Kindelberger received a personal cablegram from Lord Beaverbrook, British Minister of Aircraft Production, congratulating the company on its achievement in bettering the production schedule set for 1940 on the Harvard II type.' (*Courtesy of Rockwell International Archives*)

The classic profile of the Harvard II on the concrete at Inglewood in 1940. Between July 1941 and May 1942, 305 Harvard IIs were directly flown across the US/Canada border to equip training units of both the EATS and the BCATP, as well as SFTS squadrons where they joined RCAF Harvards. At the same time shipments to Southern Rhodesia via South African ports continued from August 1941 onwards, some 103 Mk IIs being thus despatched, while forty-seven others ultimately ended up in the Middle East. Four Mk IIs reached India but were soon expended in accidents and, finally, direct shipment of thirty-eight Mk. IIs equipped the training squadrons of the Royal New Zealand Air Force.

The Harvard Mk IIA was the equivalent of the American AT-6C. No Mark IIAs were shipped to the United Kingdom but were instead allocated to EATS units both in the Middle East (one hundred Mark IIAs) and South Africa (a total of 436 Mk. IIAs) from October 1942, and these despatches were followed by fifty-three machines to New Zealand (commencing in December 1942) and 149 to Southern Rhodesia (starting in January 1943). Later in the war the Royal Navy's Fleet Air Arm units, No. 789 Squadron at Wingfield, South Africa and No. 757 Squadron at Pattalam, Ceylon (Sri Lanka), took some. (*Courtesy of Rockwell International Archives*)

Wings for the world. The supplying of the T-6/SNJ/Harvard variants from the expanding North Amerian aircraft plant mushroomed as the war in Europe accelerated and the threat to the United States became ever greater. This 1940 photograph shows the wing racking with both USAAF and RAF markings painted up.

When the company had originally moved its operations to Inglewood, California from Dundalk, Maryland, on the basis of the Air Corps order for the original eighty-two BT-9s in November 1935, they had initially taken seventy-five key employees with them to form the nucleus of the new organisation. By January 1936, double this number of men moved into the new 158,678 square-foot factory which had the transplanted tooling and machinery installed. By 1938 this workforce had risen to 2,730 people and by 1 September 1937 to 3,400 and the factory area had expanded to almost 800,000 square-feet by November of that year.

Impressive though this expansion was with the President's call for 50,000 aircraft per annum, the two-year period between the outbreak of war in Europe and Pearl Harbor saw these totals pale into insignificance. North American increased its monthly aircraft output from seventy to 325 units, its personnel from 3,400 to 23,000 and its factory floor area to 2½ million square-feet. Even this was not to be enough. Despite further expansion at Inglewood it was clear that the plant just could not meet the flood of orders for the advanced combat trainers and other aircraft. (*Courtesy of Rockwell International Archives*)

2 The SNJ/AT-6 Development

What was to prove the final preliminary step in the progression to the AT-6 took place in 1937 and was the result of another piece of 'Dutch' Kindelberger's opportunism. The fixed landing-gear of the earlier North American trainers was looking progressively retrograde as the months went by and a main factor in limiting the aircrafts' best speed to 190 mph. The fact that both Army and Navy were now firmly wedded to North American for their standard training aircraft led the company to feel that it was time to take the next step forward.

It was a logical advance therefore to create a test model with a much improved performance, to enable the aircraft to act as an advanced trainer certainly, but also to provide the flexibility that North American required to extend the range of its potential export capabilities into general purpose and even limited fighter roles. To achieve all this a 'clean-up' design was needed which necessitated the adoption of a fully-retractable landing gear. At the same time, although the composite fuselage structure was acceptable, both the American services made it clear that all-metal construction was what they most favoured and most welcomed in future aircraft of this type. Combining both internal and external needs North American came up with the NA-26, which at its most simplistic form was a NJ-1 with retractable undercarriage.

The final step was to be the ironing out of most of the frustrating differences between the Army and Navy specifications for what was, after all, a standard Advanced Trainer aircraft for both. They could never be completely harmonious of course, as with the chartboard, the need for life-jacket stowage and, later, tailhooks and strengthening for carrier deck landings, the two services could never be absolutely compatible. But with war fast approaching they could clearly be much more amenable to each other's viewpoints and training aircraft requirements than they could ever hope to be with combat aircraft needs. Both had been for so long traditional rivals in competition for meagre Government defence funds that it took no little persuasion for the two services to harmonise their needs for the benefit of both North American, the US Government inspectors of the Bureau of Ordnance and the Allied war effort alike, but eventually it was done. And *when* it was the T-6 had finally, and absolutely, arrived!

The catalyst of this ultimate joining was of course the vast expansion programmes following the German victories in Europe and *prior* to America's entry into the war after the Japanese Navy attack at Pearl Harbor on 7 December 1941. One result of all this was a colossal expansion of the American aircraft industry and the need for brand-new factories to be built to meet the insatiable demand.

As the company history records;

> 'The large and vital trainer programme for the Army Air Corps and US Navy got underway in earnest shortly after the President's National Defense message to Congress in May of 1940. On the strength of verbal indications from Air Corps officers that a quantity of AT-6 combat trainers would be required when and if appropriations became available, the management issued a general order for the manufacture of the first group of these planes

on 28 June 1940, and work proceeded immediately. The board of directors of the corporation formally supported this action by the management in a resolution adopted at its meeting on 12 July 1940. The supporting contract was executed by the Government on 13 August 1940, calling for 637 planes of the AT-6A type (later changed to 517 AT-6A type for the Air Corps and 120 SNJ-3 type for the US Navy). Thanks to the head-start gained by the company by going ahead with production work on its own risk, the first airplane under this contract was delivered to the Air Corps on 27 September 1940, with production accelerating rapidly thereafter. The entire order for 637 planes had been completed in August 1941, just one year after the date of the contract. The first unit delivered under this contract late in September, 1940, just forty-five days after the contract was signed, was the first aeroplane delivered to the Government under a National Defense programme contract.

Shortly after this initial National Defense delivery, the company received a contract for the manufacture of 1,480 AT-6A and SNJ-3 trainers. This was the first contract undertaken by the new Dallas plant. In August of 1941, approximately four months after the first deliveries were made from the new Dallas plant, the last advanced combat trainer to be produced by the Inglewood plant under domestic contracts was delivered to the Army Air Corps. Thereafter all Army and Navy trainer deliveries were made from the Dallas plant, which then became a self-sufficient production unit capable of conducting the entire manufacturing operations on trainers.'

There were labour shortages in the Los Angeles area at that time and so North American cast about for a site for a brand-new complex, somewhere with ample space and plenty of people available to work there. Not surprisingly, their choice fell on Texas.

The company found the site it considered the most desirable next to Hensley Field, the Army Reserve airfield close to Dallas, Texas. This was also the major population centre of the American South-west. However, it was discovered that the Consolidated Aircraft Corporation was also after this site for a new plant to build their B-24 Liberator bombers. As the company history later recorded;

Although Consolidated had previously indicated to the Air Corps its desire to use this location, North American Aviation was given preference by the Air Corps. The determining factor was the pressing need for production of North American's advanced trainer; this programme was ready to go immediately, whereas Consolidated's programme was still far in the future. The Dallas plant was to be built with Defense Plant Corporation funds.

The first public announcement of selection of this location for North American's new trainer manufacturing plant was made on 17 August 1940. Ground-breaking ceremonies were held on 28 September on the bare expanse of Texas plain adjoining the Army field. The general contract for construction of the plant was not awarded until 13 November, due to delays occasioned by the D.P.C. arrangement, but events moved at top speed after the contract was awarded.

Work on the 1,022,400-square-foot plant commenced on 2 December and North American personnel began to move into the still uncompleted plant on 20 January 1941. Less than three months later, on 8 March, the first manufacturing operations commenced at the factory and on 7 April the first three AT-6A advanced trainers were turned over to the Air Corps on the occasion of the plant dedication ceremony. This was just 120 days after construction had begun.

Nor was the training programme for the new employees any less spectacular. The first class of thirty-five men was enrolled in the Dallas training school on 4 November 1940. Under the Dallas training plan, 100 new applicants were to start each fortnight on a two-week training course calculated to serve also as an entrance examination. At the end of the two-week period those who had successfully completed the course were placed on the payroll and assigned to departments for which they were best fitted, after which they began actual production work under adequate supervision as the final phase of their training.

To each plant was sent a small nucleus of supervisory personnel from among the experienced employees of the Inglewood plant. The organizational structure set up in each plant was basically similar to the Inglewood organizational structure. The work of all plants was co-ordinated by administrative staff groups in Inglewood, later to be formalized as the corporation's general office staff. As an illustration of the tremendous training job faced in these new plants, only about seventy-five men were transferred from Inglewood to the Dallas plant as its supervisory and training nucleus prior to the plant dedication in March, 1941. At the end of 1941 it was estimated that at least ninety-five per cent of the total payroll in the Dallas plant comprised native Texans who had no previous aircraft experience before being employed by North American Aviation.

Involvement in the war and rapid expansion was fine, but of course it also brought about production problems. Although the USA, as the 'Arsenal of Democracy', was completely immune from bombing attacks or indeed almost every other form of enemy intervention, the actual supply of raw materials *could* (in theory) be disrupted by the German U-boat fleet which, in 1941/42 enjoyed enormous success off American coastal areas.

This brought about the first serious alteration to the Texan's design because imported aluminium was deemed to be at a possible premium. Desirable as both Army and Navy deemed it to have all-metal fuselages for their trainers, the US War Department decided, wisely, that the needs of combat aircraft in this respect must take priority.

As a result of this decision North American brought in a series of wooden composite fuselage parts abaft of the fire-wall to compensate and lessen demand for this vital metal. Later the whole of the rear section of the fuselage was built of three-ply mahogany plywood sheeting as were the cockpit floorboards. Other internal fixtures were built of native spruce wood. This achieved a saving of 200 lbs of aluminium per aircraft. Thus composite Texans began to appear in large numbers, and, in the end, 1,243 AT-6Cs and 1,040 SNJ-4s were built to this specification. The predicted shortage of aluminium never, in fact, materialised and later production of the all-metal fuselage type was resumed as the norm.

This set the standard for further designations and that of all subsequent 'navalised' trainers. Both versions could be adapted as target tugs by the provision of cabling gear fitted on the underside of the fuselage abaft the rear cockpit.

The North American NA-88 (Army AT-6C, Navy SNJ-4) represented the ultimate amalgamation of ideas and varied little from their forebears save for certain internal alterations. Also the SNJ-4 incorporated the third machine-gun and the bomb racks carried by the Army variants which made them even more identical.

(*above*)

The US Navy, which did not rate the Wright engine very highly and had always favoured the Pratt & Whitney instead, had approved the Pratt & Whitney engined BT-10 and when they had sufficient funds, under the 1937/38 naval estimates, they immediately ordered forty of these aircraft under the designation NJ-1. Under Navy nomenclature N stood for training aircraft, J for the North American company and 1 indicted the first machine from this firm. All these NJ-1s featured the relocation of the engine airscoop from the top of the cowling to below it. None of the naval trainers were equipped with any armaments. Nor were they equipped for carrier deck landings and none had tail-hooks or strengthening.

Deliveries commenced as early as July 1937. The US Navy colour scheme at that time was bright aluminum fuselage and wings with the upper-wing surfaces a vivid orange. Those aircraft utilised for instrument training were distinguished by broad red bands around both fuselage and wings.

This photo is the NA-52 (SNJ-1), the first of a batch of sixteen such trainers given that designation on 28 September 1938. (*Courtesy of Rockwell International Archives*)

(*right*)

With a brand-new North American aircraft plant firmly established at Dallas, Texas, work got underway in earnest to try and meet the needs of North American's many customers for its outstanding product, the 120 SNJ-3s (North American NA-77, Navy Bureau of Aeronautics Requisition 1255), which had its first flight in March 1941, and the 517 AT-6As (North American NA-78, Army contract AC-15977). As we have seen, with Government prodding, these two variants were largely standardised versions of the same aircraft and the majority of the aircraft's sections, including the wings, airframe and tailplane (with the Army's triangular configuration becoming the norm), and associated nuts, bolts, seats, instrumentation, radio and other basic fittings were totally interchangeable, while visually they were were almost identical.

The wingspan of both these types was 42 feet ¼ inch, a reduction overall of 6¾ inches. In both also the fuel tanks were made removable from the centre section of the wing. Both carried the same armament of .30 Browning M2s, one a single, fixed, forward-firing weapon mounted atop the fuselage just in front of the pilot's windscreen on the starboard side, and the other a single, swivel-mounted rear-firing .30 machine-gun, with ammo box and link collector box and a stowage slot atop the aft fuselage. This latter weapon had a full, 360 degree swivelling seat for gunnery practice. Both versions featured a forward-folding rear canopy to give the rear-seat man a temporary windscreen.

Only when it came to the engines and armaments did minor differences begin, and then they were largely cosmetic for both variants used 600 hp Pratt & Whitney R-1340 power plants, the Navy version being the AN-1 (AN = Army/Navy) and the Army the 49. When later the Army in its turn also adopted the AN-1 as the AT-6B (North American NA-84), even this modest distinction vanished. (*National Archives, Washington, DC*)

In December 1941, 203 of the new advanced trainers were accepted from the Dallas plant. Thus came about the earliest nickname for the AT-6, which was appropriately enough christened the 'Texan'. Actually those aircraft built at the new Dallas plant had the suffix NT to distinguish those built at Inglewood which carried NA. (*National Archives, Washington, DC*)

The versatile T-6/SNJ was not only used for pilot training by the USAAF and the USN during the war years. They were readily adaptable for training of air gunners also. But, in addition, the same cockpit layout and reliability of the aircraft itself also lent itself to other training roles. The Royal Australian Air Force was the first to use its variant of the universal North American as a combat spotter/recce aircaft in the south-west Pacific. Post-war many other Allied nations were to adapt their T-6/ Harvard allocations for the same purpose and in Korea the AT-6 was widely used thus. But during World War II the US forces only used the rear-seat camera facilities for training of operators in this increasingly vital and essential role as this 1944 photo shows. (*National Archives, Washington, DC*)

The US Navy's SNJ-3s proved very versatile in service. For the B series
an additional .30 Browning M2 machine-gun was mounted in the
starboard wing and provision was made for underwing racks capable of
carrying four 100-lb practice bombs. These machines did not carry the
swivel seat as they were principally used for gun training which was
naturally conducted with the gun trained on the after-firing arcs.

This splendid photo shows such a configuration at a Florida base with
the trainee air gunner ready for another training sortie. (*National
Archives, Washington, DC*)

Another wartime development of the standard T-6 in the United States, this affected the last series of Harvard marks for British service also. Starting in the summer of 1943 a fresh variant appeared.

There were no external differences but there was for the first time a duplication of the most important instruments in both cockpits fore and aft. This was a most welcomed addition as far as the instructor was concerned, as he now had control over the power of the landing-gear and flaps in an emergency. Another change was to the standard electrical equipment, which, hitherto for the T-6 had been of the 12-volt system but now a change-over was made to the 24-volt system. Other internal changes were the installation of a VHF four-button communications radio and an Automatic Direction-Finding (ADF) receiver. Intitially also, a larger propeller spinner was installed on the Ds but this proved so troublesome in service that it was soon withdrawn again. These alterations were reflected by the resulting change of designation to NA-88, of which the Army and Navy designations became the AT-6D/SNJ-5. In all other respects these aircraft were repeats of the standard AT-6C/SNJ-4. In fact being intermixed on the Dallas production line 440 BT-6D and 276 SNJ-5 appeared with the composite wooden fuselage structure although the majority were of all-metal stressed-skin construction. Total output of this variant was 3,958 AT-6D and 2,198 SNJ-5. Those strengthened for carrier deck landings with tailhooks again had the suffix C added.

In the RAF these became the Harvard III and 537 were delivered. These included 143 for the Royal Navy, with twenty-five others transferred later. Thus this Mark became by far the most widely used Fleet Air Arm Harvard. The allocations of the Mark III were seventy to the EATS in Southern Rhodesia between December 1943 and July 1944, 197 to South Africa during the same period, eight-one sent to the Middle East and forty-one shipped directly to New Zealand between November 1943 and November 1944.

By 1945 few Harvard Is remained in service with the RAF, the main variant in the post-war Flying Training Command being the Harvard IIB. The Harvard II was one of the mainstays of the wartime training programme in Canada, and the Mks. IIA, IIB and III saw service mainly in Southern Rhodesia.

This Harvard III is 7111 of the South African Air Force, taken in April 1987 near Cape Town, and features the then standard trainer markings of red tail and rear fuselage, engine cowling and leading edge and wing-tip with the standard yellow blocked out number. She was one of the Central Flying School's formation team at that time, hence the red strips adorning the leading edges of the wings. (*Courtesy Arthur Pearcy, Sharnbrook*)

Among the earliest of the 'Warbird' restorations of the SNJ workhorse post-war was this splendid example photographed by Jim Larsen in 1976. Its proud owner was Ben Harrison of Seattle, Washington, USA. The aircraft itself was painted in the colours of the Pensacola Training School during the period 1940-41. Not only was the colour scheme authentic but much painstaking work went into the rest of the restoration.

The entire airframe and the engine itself were also carefully overhauled and refurbished with the same devotion to detail. Many remanufactured or new parts had, perforce, to be incorporated although the bulk of the original airframe was maintained complete. The cockpit instrumentation was restored to its original positioning and brought up to factory-freshness. However, some compromise had to made to fit modern flying conditions and some new lightweight electronic gear was substituted for the old navigation equipment to fit 1970's laws.

The feature of the swivelling rear seat for rear gunnery training was one point in case for the US Navy's SNJ-3s were often used for this role. None of the original flexible mounted machine-guns could be fitted but of course the unusual rear canopy mechanism and seat functions were retained in Ben's Warbird.

Fully airworthy again N2864D was one of the pioneer efforts which showed just what could be done and set the trend towards T-6 restoration and revival after decades in which the more glamorous (and expensive) fighter types had predominated the civil scene. (*Courtesy Jim Larsen collection*)

The Hamilton Standard two-bladed propeller was fitted to the standard production T-6s no matter which powerplant the Army and Navy initially decided upon. Standardisation was not to be achieved until well after the war had got underway.

Thus the first BC-1 prototype took to the air on 11 February 1938, only a day after the first flight of the BT-14. Engined by the 550 hp Pratt & Whitney R-1340-47 Wasp radial, trials and evaluations resulted in minor alterations to the rudder, it being made larger with the bottom edge being squared-off to aid directional control. The streamlining effect of the new under-carriage, plus the new engine, combined to give the BC-1 a top speed of 209 mph.

Impressed, the Army placed an initial contract for 180 BC-1 trainers. Of these, three dozen were actually completed as instrument training aircraft and given the designation BC-1I (I for Instrument). In these aircraft hoods were fitted to the rear cockpit for blind-flying instruction. They could also be identified by the manually controlled radio loop-antenna which was carried abaft

the landing-gear on the underside of the wing.

Progress was also made on the other home-front at this time, for the US Navy also trialed and evaluated the BC-1 throughout the summer of 1938. The Navy was also switching over to monoplane aircraft, with fighters like the Grumman Wildcat, dive-bombers like the Vought Vindicator and torpedo planes like the Douglas Devastator, and with improved models of all three types on the drawing boards (Hellcat, Dauntless and Avenger). They were thus very interested in the new advance trainer concept.

It was Navy needs that saw the final stage of the metamorphosis completed, for they stipulated in their September specification to the company that the all-metal fuselage, as in the BT-14, was an essential feature. This was wedded to the retractable landing gear and armament of the BC-1 and the adoption of the 500 hp Pratt & Whitney R-1340-6 engine in place of the existing powerplant. North American quickly complied with all these wishes and the resulting aircraft, the NA-52, was delivered towards the end of the year for trials. (*Courtesy of Rockwell International Archives*)

Here a large formation of Navy SNJ-3s head out on a mass flight under lowering clouds and thunderheads in 1943. All-weather training over water and long-distance navigation were of course a must for US Navy carrier aircrew due to join carrier Task Forces for the closing actions of the Pacific War against Japan. The all-metal construction of the Dash-3 was regarded as one of its strengths early on. However, strangely, in the early months of American involvement in the shooting war there were doubts about the wisdom of this. (*National Archives, Washington, DC*)

The US Navy made extensive use of its SNJ trainers throughout World War II. With the bulk of the available manpower serving at the front and overseas, the US Navy like most combatants, relied increasingly on female recruits to keep the aircraft flying.

Here a bunch of Navy WAVES, (left to right) Inez Waits, S1/C AMM; Lucille H. Henderson, S1/C AMM and Mary Anne Gasser, S1/C AMM, Helen Adams, 3/C and Leona Curry, S1/C AMM, all Aviation Metal Smiths, are seen checking out an SNJ engine in the assembly and repair department of the Naval Air Station at Jacksonville, Florida, prior to its take-off. The ladies are posed for the camera around the 500 hp Pratt & Whitney R-1340-6 engine which drove the two-bladed controllable-pitch propeller. The first SNJ had been delivered in May 1939 and thousands rolled off the production lines in the years that followed, gradually becoming standardised with the Army's T-6. (*National Archives, Washington DC*)

(*left*)

When the Navy came to adapt fifty-five of the original SNJs for carrier deck landings at NAS Pensacola by the installation of a tailhook, the suffix C (for Carrier) was added to their designations and that of all subsequent 'navalised' trainers. Both versions could be further adapted as target tugs by the provision of cabling gear fitted on the underside of the fuselage abaft the rear cockpit.

The North American NA-88 (Army AT-6C, Navy SNJ-4) represented the ultimate amalgamation of ideas and varied little from their forebears save for certain internal alterations. Also the SNJ-4 incorporated the third machine-gun and the bomb racks carried by the Army variants which made them even more identical. (*National Archives, Washington, DC*)

'Texan Away!' A flight-deck scene from the late war period.

In America the US Navy's SNJ-5Cs modified for carrier landing training with navigation tables and tailhooks had continued in service working from the training carriers (TCVs) USS *Sable* (IX. 81, formerly the mercantile *Greater Buffalo*) and USS *Wolverine* (IX. 64, formerly the mercantile *Seeandbee*). These were Great Lakes paddle-tankers modified like escort carriers by the fitting of 500 foot-long wooden flight-decks. They had been converted in 1942 for this role and worked out of Chicago on Lake Michigan steadily until they were finally scrapped in 1947 and 1948. The SNJs were not based on these vessels of course but flew out to them from the Glenview Naval Air Station in Illinois for each day's training. A proper seagoing escort carrier, the former British *Charger* (CVE. 30, formerly the mercantile *Rio de la Plata*) had operated in a similar capacity off the Pensacola navy base, on the Florida coast during the same period. The post-war replacement of these training carriers were the two former light carriers USS *Saipan* (CVL 48) and USS *Wright* (CVL. 49), completed in 1946 and 1947 respectively and they continued in service in the training role until the advent of jet trainers made them redundant in the late 1950s. They were capable of thirty-three knots as against the earlier ships' best of eighteen knots which made for more realistic deck operations for the SNJs. (*US National Archives, Washington DC*)

(below)
An undignified re-entry to the world. Carrier-based operation was a hazardous enough operation out at sea during wartime conditions, but for many rookie pilots getting their SNJ off the giant runways of the Navy flying schools sometimes proved just as awesome until one got the hang of things. This is one such SNJ that went 'into the drink' and had to be recovered by the salvage men – it was more-or-less in one piece. (*Courtesy of the late Herb Cook, INTERCOM, Fort Worth*)

(*left*)
A US Navy SNJ 'Winds up' in preparation for take-off from the flight deck of the USS *Long Island* (ACV 1) used for training purposes in the war. Pilot qualification period included deck take-offs and landings and this photograph was taken on 28 January 1943. (*US National Archives, Washington DC*)

A beautiful study of a restored US Marine Corps SNJ-2 (N5208V) in the original colour scheme belonging to VM-308 at Pensacola, Florida, training base, owned and flown by Frank Compton.

Early in 1940 the US Navy was once more active and had contracted for an additional sixty-one SNJ-2s (North American NA-65). These were really SNJ-1s with a few minor changes. The SNJ-2 had its maiden flight on 20 March 1940 and was powered by the 600 hp Pratt & Whitney R-1340-36 radial again with a two-bladed prop. This combination gave the aircraft a best speed of 214 mph with a ceiling of over 24,000 feet. Modifications involved the removal of the carburettor air scoop to the port side of the fuselage abaft the engine cowl, which itself had a larger ring fitting. An additional vent scoop was located below the cowl due to the repositioning of the oil cooler to the port side of the engine.

The SNJ-2s could be distinguished by their retention of the rounded rudder form and from the clumsy and awkward positioning of the large radio antenna mast which was plonked slap in the pilot's line of vision on top of the fuselage abaft the engine cowling. Close-up the Navy's standards of fitments evidenced themselves in leather headrests and the need for a chart board for the pilot for over-water navigation. The initial order for three dozen aircraft was for the Naval Reserve units and was followed by a repeat order to twenty-nine more as Congressional funding became available for Roosevelt's 'Two-Ocean Navy' following the fall of France. (*Courtesy Dr Ira Chart*)

A unique aerial photograph of a unique aircraft. The one and only T-6 with an in-line engine!

The in-line engine had been heavily promoted by Fairchilds before the war and they presented several advantages of this type over the radial. Such engines gave a low profile forward and thus the pilot had a much improved view out of his forward windscreen, essential for high-speed fighter tactics as epitomised by the British Supermarine Spitfire and German Messerschmitt Me. 109 in the Battle of Britain, the aerial combat which became every air force's bench-mark after 1940. Such in-line engines had the natural advantages of smoother running and less vibration with their balanced crankshaft-connection rod arrangements, which equated with less wear-and-tear on both machine and pilot. Also, because the in-line engine's prop shaft would always be the physically highest point of the engine, a larger diameter propeller could be mounted for more efficiency, or, alternately, with the same-size propeller a shorter undercarriage could be utilised, and this equated with less weight and better landing visibility.

Weighing all these factors in the balance the go-ahead was given by the Army for the experiment to be conducted. The result was the XAT-6E. FEC's Haggerstown, Maryland, airfield was the test-bed site for the work and here a 575 hp Ranger air-cooled inverted 12-cylinder SGV-770-D4 in line engine, which drove a two-bladed propeller fitted with a spinner and which was

supercharged for high-altitude flights, was installed in an AT-6D (No 42-84241). This engine gave 520 hp for take-off, 80 hp less than the Pratt & Whitney R-1340. The two-feet longer nose required by the Ranger meant the complete rebuilding of the airframe forward of the fire-wall and strict rebalancing to compensate. Overall length was thirty-one feet.

Work was complete at Haggerstown during 1944 and the XAT-6E was then transported to Elgin Army Air Force Base in Florida and air tested against a conventional 600-hp radial-engined AT-6D.

Comparison of test figures showed the following results. At sea-level the XAT-6E had a bare 3 mph speed advantage over the AT-6D, 196 mph against 193 mph. The higher the altitude the greater this advantage became, being 19 mph at 10,000 feet (220 mph against 201 mph) and 59 mph at 20,000 feet where the in-line continued to increased to 231 mph while the radial fell off dramatically to 172 mph. At 22,000 feet no figures were given for the conventional Texan but the supercharged XAT-6E was clocking 236 mph. Final testing pushed the service ceiling up to 30,000 feet and registered a top speed of 244 mph.

The Ranger-engined XAT-6E was therefore proven to be both the fastest and the highest-flying of all the Texans, but only the one prototype was ever built and no production orders followed. (*National Archives, Washington, DC*)

43

The USS *Wolverine* (IX. 64, formerly the mercantile *Seeandbee*) was a sister ship of the *Sable*. They were both Great Lakes paddle-tankers modified like escort carriers by the fitting of 500 foot-long wooden flight-decks. They had been converted in 1942 for this role and worked out of Chicago on Lake Michigan steadily until they were finally scrapped in 1947 and 1948. The SNJs were not based on this vessel of course but flew out of them from the Glenview Naval Air Station in Illinois for each day's training.

Taken off Chicago, Illinois in December 1942, this photo shows crewmen working on a deckload of SNJs whose engines have been warmly muffled to keep out the bitter cold of the Great Lakes in winter. (*US National Archives, Washington, DC*)

The control panel in the after (instructor's) cockpit of SN-2J G-6. The original caption for this photograph read as follows:- 'From this control panel in the rear cockpit, instructors can temporarily 'upset' instruments in the cadet's front cockpit to simulate emergencies during flight training in the new XSN2J-1 trainer developed by North American Aviation, Inc., for the US Navy. The Navy has ordered the plane for evaluation in connection with its modernized pilot training programme.' (*Courtesy of Rockwell International Archives*)

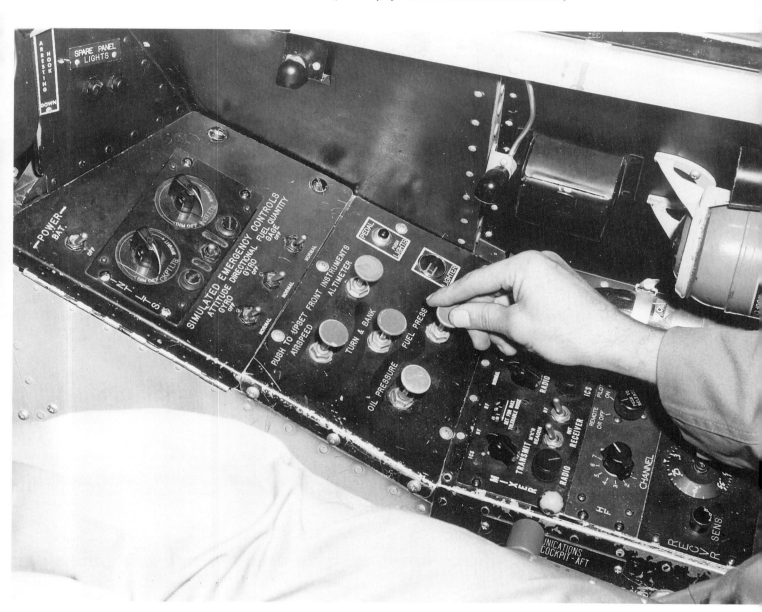

(*left*)
The USS *Wolverine* (IX. 64, formerly the mercantile *Seeandbee*) was a sister ship of the *Sable*. Here the decks have been swept of snow as the carrier operates just north of the city of Chicago, Illinois, in December 1942. As an SNJ (6972) runs up its engine, deck crew stand-by with fire extinguishers, 'just in case'. (*US National Archives, Washington, DC*)

Many famous pilots have cut their teeth on the Harvard or the T-6 down the years. This photograph shows one of the most famous of them all. His Royal Highness, The Duke of Edinburgh is pictured here 'Going Solo' for the first time on his advanced pilots' course in a Harvard. The photo was taken by Charles E. Brown in another Harvard piloted by Flight Lieutenant C.R. Gordon, the Duke's flying instructor, over Windsor Castle. Air traffic conditions from Heathrow were not then what they have become today obviously! (*Charles E. Brown photo courtesy of R.C. Sturtivant Archives*)

3 The Versatile Harvard

Before moving on to cover the final wartime developments of the American versions of the Texan and the several variants adapted for other roles than training, we must retrace our steps a while to examine the equally large British and Commonwealth involvement with the type.

Resident British representatives arrived at the Inglewood plant during July, and the first Harvard produced was test flown from the adjoining airfield on 28 September 1938. After the completion of test flight and the formal acceptance by the British of this machine in the middle of October, the aircraft was shipped from Los Angeles aboard the SS *Lochatrine* of the Furness Line, sailing on 24 October by way of the Panama Canal to Liverpool. A company pilot from North American had been sent to England to conduct the initial flights and he was joined by a staff of mechanics whose duty it was to assist the British in uncrating, assembling and testing the Harvards as they arrived from overseas.

The enthusiasm for the Harvard by some British instructors was rather muted as it was a complex aircraft to understand after the simple trainers hitherto in use, like the gentle de Havilland Tiger Moth and such. It also had vicious spin tendencies which could fatally catch out novice pilot and veteran teacher alike. Nonetheless it was instantly recognised as a distinct advance on what had gone before. One anonymous RAF Chief Flying Instructor was quoted in the New York *Sun* newspaper as being wildly over the top about his new charge.

> 'What I think so good is their marvellous cockpit layout. It's like a car. In some aeroplanes the controls seem to be put anywhere there is space. The result is knobs, buttons and levers everywhere; under the seat, behind your back, over your head, under your arms. The Harvard trainer gives the impression that the designer sat down and made a plan of his controls before he began to build his machine. It was decided that one place was just right for every instrument and gadget and there it went. We call it the Yankee layout.'

The desperate war situation and the loss of western Europe finally awoke most Americans to their own isolation in an ever-hostile world. This enabled President Roosevelt to push through the historic Lend-Lease deal under the terms of which US Military funding purchased huge numbers of both American and foreign-built aircraft. Under these contracts the US Army or Navy then Lend-Leased these self-same aircraft, under American designations and serial numbers but with foreign markings and serial numbers actually factory painted on them, to 'deserving' nations. Officially the aircraft would then be returned by the countries in question to the United States at the end of hostilities. The majority of the British and Commonwealth Harvards were, although many others had been crashed, wrecked, scrapped and also transferred to other countries in the interim, even some going back to the USAAF. Keeping track of all these 'paper exchanges' is a nightmare best left to the super-fanatical enthusiast – suffice it that this very generous ploy worked well for Britain when she needed it most. Under the terms of the new Lend-Lease Bill the RAF contracted for 747 AT-6Cs as Harvard IIAs. Another 1,500 Harvard IIs built in Canada were funded by the US Army. British contracts had reached 1,100 before Lend-

Lease and total deliveries to British Commonwealth Air Forces exceeded 5,000. This included 400 Mk. I, 1,173 Mk. II, 726 Mk. IIA, 2,485 Mk. IIB and 351 Mk. III.

Meantime, on 3 December 1938 the first aircraft of the initial order had arrived from Liverpool docks for trials and tests at the Aeroplane and Armament Experimental Establishment at Martlesham Heath. From these tests the British Pilots Notes were prepared. Number 7000 was the first of the many Harvards that were to serve in British and Commonwealth air forces. The Harvard Is were serialled N 7000-N 7199 and P 5783-5982. Later versions ranged between AH 185 and KG 309, delivered in 1944.

The Harvard was to remain standard equipment for the RAF's Flying Training Schools for more than sixteen years. Unfortunately N 7000 was almost immediately written-off when, on 16 February 1939, a spin caused it to crash at Eyke, close to Woodbridge in Suffolk, killing both crew members. Its replacement N 7001 had already arrived at Martlesham the month before and N 7002 arrived at the Central Flying School the same month for instructors to gauge the new aircraft. The Flying Training Schools also began to receive their due allocations soon after, the first being twelve to FTS at Spitalgate, Grantham in January.

Outwardly, if not internally, the British modifications were modest. Following the precedent set by Yale the new trainer took the name Harvard quite naturally. The radio equipment was the main alteration in service, along with some instrumentation and the seats were altered so that seat-pack parachutes could be carried. This meant the radio mast in front of the cockpit was deleted while a large heating muffler was fitted to the exhaust on the starboard side to heat the cockpit in Britain's bleak skies.

Pre-war shipments had progressed steadily from Inglewood.

> 'Export records were shattered from time to time on the British and French contracts. For example, on 31 March 1939, twenty crated Harvard airplanes were shipped from Los Angeles harbor aboard a single vessel bound for Liverpool. This shipment then constituted the largest quantity of airplanes of a single type ever to leave the United States on one vessel. The last airplane of the initial RAF contract for 200 airplanes was shipped from Los Angeles harbor on 20 May 1939, less than eleven months after the company had received the contract from the British Air Ministry. Meanwhile the plant was busy producing 200 additional Harvard airplanes, which had been added to the contract.'

It is relative to include here a look at the French Government order for what was basically the same aircraft, because ultimately many of them were later to enter service with the RAF and not the French Air Force. The initial contract from the French government for the manufacture of 230 NA-57 basic trainer type aeroplanes (similar to the BT-14) was approved on 14 February 1939. The contract also provided for twenty-seven equivalent airframes as spare parts at a total cost in excess of seven million US dollars. The first production article was accepted at the factory by representatives of the French government in April. Just as the British orders, the airframes were crated at the Inglewood factory, trucked to Los Angeles harbour and shipped to France on vessels of a French steamship company.

> 'The first NA-57 trainer was flown at Châteaudun, France, on 29 June 1939, by a company test pilot despatched from England for that purpose. Soon thereafter a staff of factory mechanics was established at Châteaudun to assist the Armée de l'Air in uncrating and assembling the aircraft. Export shipping records established in the shipment of Harvards to Great Britain were shattered on 31 July 1939, when a total of forty crated NA-57 trainers were shipped out of New Orleans, which had been substituted as the port of embarkation in order to rush deliveries, destined for Le Havre aboard the French Line SS *Louisiane*.

The typical two-seat Harvard with the all-metal stressed-skin construction had a wingspan of 42ft ¼ inches, a length of 28 feet 11⅞ inches, and a height of 11 feet 8½ inches and a total wing area of 253 square feet. Weight empty was 4,158 lb, loaded 5,250 lb, maximum speed was 205 mph at 5,000 feet, cruising speed 170 mph. Initial climb was 1,350 feet per minute and it had a range of 750 miles, an endurance of 3.9 hours and a service ceiling of 21,500 feet.

The equivalent to the American AT-6A, the Harvard IIB was licence-built in Canada by Noorduyn Aviation Company of Cartierville, near Montreal, Quebec, who produced 2,798 of them. At its peak Canadian production rate reached 113 per month. 1,500 of these were subsequently turned over to the US Army Air Corps which, because of their different instruments, were designated as the AT-16. The Canadian-built Mark IIBs formed the greater bulk of all British-flown Harvards and these began to arrive at EATS, BCATP and Canadian SFTS units from May 1942 onward. In all, 639 Mark IIBs were delivered up to the end of 1943. Seventy-two of the Canadian allocated Mark IIBs were subsequently shipped to the UK in March 1944 where they joined hordes of the same type which had been shipped over from April 1943 onward via Speke, near Liverpool for initial assembly and ultimately to the various Maintenance Units (MUs) across the country where they were stored pending allocation to squadrons. In fact there was an over-supply by this period of the war and some never saw anything other than storage and scrapping. Others were re-allocated to the USAAF and other Allied nations during and after the war's end.

Foreign deliveries of the Mark IIB included 507 to the RAF in India from February 1943 onward, (seventeen more were lost at sea) and forty-two modified for target towing sent to the Middle East in January 1945. In the British Fleet Air Arm the Harvard III was the variant that featured most strongly, along with a few Mk. IIBs.

Here a North American Harvard IIB (FE992 – G-BDAM) is seen revving up on the ground at RNAS Yeovilton on 19 December 1985. (*Fleet Air Arm Museum, Yeovilton*)

The British aspect of the North American trainer programme involved those aircraft built for the Royal Air Force (and other air forces of the Empire) which were constructed in the American plants, and also numerous others which were licence-built both in Canada and Australia.

In April 1938, the newly-formed British Purchasing Commission arrived in Washington DC empowered to spend 25 million dollars with which to purchase vitally needed American aircraft types to equip the expanding Royal Air Force. The first aircraft they selected for purchase was the North American NA-49 and, on 22 June 1938, they placed an order on behalf of the British Air Ministry for 200 Harvard I type aeroplanes (plus twenty-five equivalent airframes in spare parts) under Contract Number 791588/38 from the Inglewood plant. The total cost of this order was six-and-a-half million US dollars. The Harvard I (commencing with serial number N 7000) was the British version of the US Army Air Corps' BC-1 of 1937, and the initial contract for two hundred was completed in June 1939. The RAF acquired 200 as Harvard Is and the RCAF received thirty. These became the Harvard Mk.I and were to be fitted with some British instrumentation on their arrival in the United Kingdom.

With home orders at that time thin on the ground, the North American concern went out of its way to please this important new client. As it later recorded, 'When the first order for 200 of North American's BC-1 type combat training airplanes was placed by the British Purchasing Commission in the summer of 1938, the company's engineering department shattered all design records in revising the basic airplane to meet British requirements and accommodate British equipment. Although 990 of the original 2,200 design drawings required changes for this rush export project, the engineers performed their work so rapidly that the first completed airplane was test-flown in England only 120 days after design work had started, and so well that the British almost immediately ordered additional quantities of the sturdy Harvard trainer, as it was called'.

This early photo was taken in the summer of 1940 and shows instructor and trainee boarding their mount at a Canadian airfield under the Empire Air Training Scheme while one of the ground crew makes some last minute adjustments for the benefit of the cameraman! (*Courtesy of the Canadian Forces Photographic Unit, Ottawa*)

In the late 1940s eight RCAF Harvards were sold to Turkey, seventeen to France, one to Italy and one to the RCN. Similarly of the 494 Mark IIBs Sweden bought 142, the Royal Netherlands Air Force forty-nine, the Royal Danish Air Force four, the Royal Norwegian Air Force seven, the Swiss Air Force two and the Israeli Defence Force one.

That still left many hundreds in service with the RCAF itself and they continued to serve for many years as trainers until replaced by the new jet generation. Other uses were found for them by the services of course.

Between 1962 and 1964 the most famous unit was the RCAF's 'Goldilocks' aerobatic team which put on impressive displays all across Canada. The Harvard remained on the RCAF's inventory until 1965. On 19 May of that year, at No. 4 FTS, Penhold, Alberta, Flight Lieutenant J.A. Cratchley and his student, Officer Cadet J.W. Lussier, flew Harvard 20384 into history on the last training mission on this aircraft type with the RCAF.

Here the distinctive gold Harvard IV, with its red flash and bird-of-prey fuselage scheme, stands out boldly in this unique aerial view. (*Courtesy Jim Larsen, Kirklands, Washington*)

The first fateful steps! A young Canadian pilot walks out with his instructor to take his first flight at an RCAF training base in 1964. The versatility of the T-6/Harvard concept enabled this reliable machine to carry on in its basic training mode long after the advent of jet trainers for advanced duties and ensured that it was one of the most long-serving military aircraft of any era. (*Courtesy CFPU, Ottawa, Canada*)

(above)

Early wartime colour photography is extremely rare but Harold Bennett took this photograph of a wartime training flight over Canada which is notable for its clarity considering the age of the negative. The Harvard Mark II in the foreground, AJ-930, (Construction number 76.3900) was originally built as part of the French Government's order for 450 machines but was taken-over by the RAF on completion in 1940. She spent some time with 39, 34 and 13 Service Flying Training Schools in Canada before being transferred to the Royal Canadian Air Force. (*Courtesy R.C. Sturtivant*)

(below)

The faithful old Harvards were finally phased out of the Flying Training Schools with the introduction of Vampire T.II jet trainers in 1954/55.

It was not until 23 March 1955, however, that the very last RAF pilots were to gain their 'wings' by qualifying on the North American Harvard trainer. This event took place at No. 3 FTS Feltwell. This was not, however, the end of Harvard quasi-military service in Britain, as for long after this they continued to fly in Home Command's University Air Squadrons. A few lingered on as communications aircraft, while others saw combat operations against the Mau Mau uprising in Kenya and the communist insurgents in the Malayan jungle.

Among the Harvards to fly on in the United Kingdom was this veteran AT-6C Mark IIA, the former 88-10108, 41-33365, EX392, here carrying its old South African Air Force marking of 7185 in the yellow panel, as well as the civilian registration of G-BGOU. This aircraft was registered to A.P. Snell in January 1983 when she received these markings after formerly belonging to Europworld International at Biggin Hill. She is seen here taxying up the runway at West Malling airfield on 26 August 1985 on one of her last flights. On 7 September of the same year this machine crashed at Bourn killing her owner-pilot. (*RAF Museum, Hendon, London*)

Shown here in a somewhat world-weary condition is an ex-Royal Canadian Air Force Harvard IV, CF-URH (20367). She was rescued from oblivion and is pictured here at Long Beach, California, in July 1968, prior to her re-building.

The Canadian Harvard Aircraft Association is another outstanding organisation with a large, and very knowledgeable, membership. In 1989 they had five machines, a mix of North American, Noorduyn and Canadian Car and Foundry-built types. There is also the Canadian Warplanes Heritage Group, Ontario, which currently have four flyable Harvards in their team and they also boast the only T-6G in Canada. The CHAA have a very wise and enthusiastic chronicler in Doug MacPhail of Dundas.

Just across the US border, a trio of ex-Spanish T-6s work together over the Lake Michigan area, piloted by Dick Hansen, Russ Cook and Ron Kuhny. (*Courtesy Nick Williams Collection*)

A refined version of the NA-55 (BC-1A) was ordered by Great Britain as the war got under way in earnest. On 17 November 1939 some six hundred were ordered and designated Harvard IIs. A further British order followed specifically for the Royal Canadian Air Force, then a separate order for the RCAF, while undelivered orders to France were also taken-over under the same designation. This gave a grand total of 1,275 Harvard IIs. They carried a wing-mounted gun, and the engine exhaust was muffled to aid in cockpit heating in northern climes.

Shown here is one of the Harvard IIs given a NA-75 charge number on 3 June 1940. This was one of the direct-purchase order from the British Government for the Royal Canadian Air Force for 100 machines (Serials 75-3048 to 3057 and 75-3418 to 3507). (*Courtesy of Rockwell International Archives*)

Line-up of Harvards at a snow-bound Canadian flying school in the Toronto area in the winter of 1941. While the majority have adopted the standard RAF Yellow overall paint scheme, at least one (2557) has the early two-tone scheme.

The large orders received from both Britain and France in 1938/39 enabled the company to proceed with its expansion plans with a great degree of confidence. By the outbreak of war in Europe, North American had almost completed the first two British contracts, totalling 400 trainers, and were well on the way with the French order for 230 of the same type.

This initial order was soon increased. On 11 November 1939 an order was placed for 600 Harvard IIs (BC-1A/NA-55). A second direct-purchase British order followed for the Royal Canadian Air Force, a total of 100 Harvard IIs (NA-75s) being procured. As with the Yale, on the fall of France, Britain was able to step in and secure some 450 NA-76s ordered by that nation. British equipment replaced the French but the radio mast remained *in situ* in these machines after delivery. They were rated as Harvard IIs.

Yet a further batch of Harvard IIs (NA-81s) was ordered on 11 July 1940, this being a combined RAF/RCAF order for 125 aircraft. However, not all saw service with these air forces for some of these were appropriated by the USAAC before delivery with only insignificant alterations to them. (*Courtesy of Canadian Forces Photographic Unit, Ontario*)

What was to prove the last aeroplane under the second French contract for 230 basic trainers was not completed until August 1940. 'Since German troops had entered Paris on 14 June and France had sued for peace on 17 June, the undelivered portion of this contract was taken-over by the British government, and the aeroplanes were delivered to Canada.'

For the RAF personnel from the very first flight with No. 3 SFTS, at Grantham, what one Canadian history described as 'the Harvard's characteristic rasping note' was to become a familiar sound over airfields across the whole world and more than fifty years on it is just as distinctive. This highly individual grating was caused by the direct-drive prop with its high tip speeds and earned the T-6 yet another of its many epithets, that of the 'Noisy North American'. However much it jarred on the ears it is a sound that is still well remembered by a hundred thousand novice pilots and worried instructors, from Brazil to Minsk, from Medicine Hat to Queensland and from Montrose to Alipore. It is never forgotten by all who flew it.

Here a flight of three Harvards (2928, 2631 and 2917) are seen over Canada in 1941. Note the variations in their identity markings. (*Courtesy of Canadian Forces Photographic Unit, Ontario*)

North American Harvard IIs of 20 Service Flying Training School lined up at Cranbourne, near Salisbury (Harare) Southern Rhodesia (Zimbabwe) during the war. The unit was equipped with Mark IIs from the autumn of 1941 until the end of the war, about 114 reaching them and fellow schools in that country during this period, of which forty were lost through crashes during the Empire Air Training Scheme programmes.

At the end of the war a further thirty-one Mark IIs were scrapped in situ in November 1945. Of the thirty odd survivors a dozen were sold to the Southern Rhodesian Air Force in February 1949 and carried on with their duties in the training role for many years before being sold on again. (*RAF Museum, Hendon, London*)

Crash! Where novice pilots were concerned not all flights in the Harvard had happy endings. Some errors were paid for dearly.

The wrecked remains of a Harvard II (AJ715 E) of 20 Service Flying Training School after an horrific crash at a farm near Salisbury, Southern Rhodesia, (now Zimbabwe) on 4 April 1942. Normally based at Cranbourne, this particular flight was made from the Pendennis Relief Landing Ground. (*RAF Museum, Hendon, London*)

Ready for the off!

A posed for the camera view of two RAF flying personnel seated aboard a North American Harvard II (DC) of 11 Service Flying Training School, Royal Canadian Air Force, taken at Yorkton airfield, in December 1941.

By March 1941, Inglewood had passed the 1,000 quantity mark on the Harvard for the British and Empire Air Forces, which at that time, was an all-time record for a single model of airplane. Although identified as a single model, these were not 1,000 identical planes, however. Actually there were 2,500 drawing changes made after the first Harvard was produced, and among the 1,000 combat trainers there were actually more than twenty-five different models, each varying from the others in some major or minor detail of construction.

Between July 1941 and May 1942, 305 Harvard IIs were directly flown across the US/Canada border to equip training units of both the EATS and the BCATP, as well as SFTS squadrons where they joined RCAF Harvards. At the same time shipments to Southern Rhodesia via South African ports continued from August 1941 onward, some 103 Mk IIs being thus despatched, while forty-seven others ultimately ended up in the Middle East. Four Mk IIs reached India but were soon expended in accidents and, finally, direct shipment of thirty-eight Mk.IIs equipped the training squadrons of the Royal New Zealand Air Force.

Three Harvards of the Royal Canadian Air Force over a snowy backdrop in 1941.

When the fighter operational training units were redesignated as OTUs in March 1940 their establishment strength already included numerous Harvard Is. Finally, with the setting-up in the same month of the British Commonwealth Air Training Plan (BCATP) in Canada and the Empire Air Training Scheme (EATS) in Southern Rhodesia (now known as Zimbabwe), direct shipping to 20 and 20 Service Flying Training Schools (SFTS) from the States was undertaken. This was accelerated when the whole of the British training effort was shifted there in July of the same year, some 216 British-based Harvards being packed for transhipment at Cardiff and Odiham for the southern African destination, with a further eight going to the Middle East. Very few Harvards remained flying over the UK although units like 15 SFTS at Lossiemouth continued to feature Harvard Is until April of the following year. The Harvard, in all its guises, was the second most numerous aircraft type to be used in the BCATP.

Meanwhile Harvard IIs were arriving in both Canada, where twenty equipped the BCATP units and eight more in the UK, being followed by a further six (with another six going down with their ship after a U-boat attack in the North Atlantic *en route*). Two of these were subsequently allocated to the USAAF and the rest joined the Mk.Is.

No obvious place to put down! Both pilot and instructor had more than the scenery on their minds during this mid-50s training flight.

Set against the magnificent backdrop of the Rocky Mountains this duo of Royal Canadian Air Force Harvards (20248 and 20293) come from the Canadian Car and Foundry-built batch of 555 Mark IVs which were built from 1951 onward and were the Canadian-built version of the T-6G. They could be readily identified by the small type ADF mounting carried astern of the cockpit. They also had an exhaust shroud on the right-hand side not visible in this photo. (*Courtesy of the Canadian Government, Ottawa*)

In Canada the Harvard equalled the longevity of the American T-6. The first three had been received in Vancouver in July 1939 and had been accepted at Camp Borden in August. They were used as advanced trainers at Nos 1, 2, 6, 8, 9 and 13 RCAF Service Flying Training Schools at Camp Borden, Ottawa, Dunnville, Moncton, Summerside and St. Hubert. In addition they were used by Nos 31, 32 and 39 RAF SFTSs at Kingston, Moose Jaw and Swift Current. They were still working as standard equipment in the summer of 1963 with No.2 Flying Training School at Moose Jaw and No. 3 FTS at Penhold. A total of 2,063 Harvards were eventually used by the RCAF. Trainee pilots were initially given instruction at schools like St. Kitts, Ontario, receiving sixty-five hours of basic training on the Fleet Finch and the de Havilland Tiger Moth, before moving on to the Harvard. In Canada, Harvards were also used by Nos 14, 111, 115, 123, 126, 127, 129, 130, 132, 133, 135, 163, 166 and 167 RCAF Squadrons for training and communications work. In all some 11,000 Canadian and 8,000 Allied pilots were trained in Canada on Harvards under CATS.

All the 224 Mark II former RAF Harvards that remained behind when the CATS had been pulled out of Canada in 1944 became RCAF property. When Canada became part of NATO in August 1949, a further 6,000 pilots learned to fly in Canadian Harvards. Allocations were also made to NATO allies. The Canadians also adopted the T-6G conversions and this machine of the Royal Canadian Navy in its distinctive markings was one of the last of the type to see active service there. (*Canadian Forces Photographic Unit, Ottawa*)

Zimbabwe (Southern Rhodesia before Independence) had twelve Harvard Mark IIs as its initial aerial strength on the formation of its air force in February 1949. They purchased nine more from South Africa in April of the same year and a further eleven from the UK in August 1951. These were later exchanged for Mark IIAs.

In RAF service a pair of Harvard Is flew in Southern Rhodesia until November 1945, while the very last two saw service in the Middle East in January 1947. Three Harvard Mark IIs survived in the Rhodesian Air Training Group until December 1949, before being 'Struck Off Charge'. With the Mark IIA, a solitary survivor served at Deversoir until November 1950, others lingered on until sold abroad as above. The last Harvards to be used of the Mark III type were those flying with the Royal Navy Reserve Squadrons, which used them until 1956. The final Harvard IIBs survived in University Squadrons and at Hong Kong until 1957, while the last one serving with an FTS was working from Feltwell prior to April 1955. Two of this Mark (FT 375 and KF 183) still survive and serve the RAF at Boscombe Down in flyable condition.

One of these aircraft (7185 G-BGOU) is shown here with its original markings, taxying at West Malling airfield on 26 August 1985. (*RAF Museum, Hendon*)

This Harvard was one of the latest flying originals and was unique. It is the Royal New Zealand Air Force Harvard (NZ934) which was presented to the Royal Australian Air Force Museum.

This former RNZAF Harvard had been grounded since 1962 and was stored at Shepparton Museum of Aviation. It was restored in 1988 and flew again in March of that year in Australia. Give the name *City of Canberra* the restoration work cost some 80,000 Australian dollars. Unfortunately this aircraft was involved in a bad crash at Canberra airport on 9 July 1989, blocking the intersection of two of the main runways there. Apparently the landing gear collapsed during a circuit flight touch-down and the Harvard finished up on its belly. The pilot and passenger were both unharmed but extensive damage was done to the wings, undercarriage and propeller of the Harvard itself.

At the time of writing it is hoped that the machine can be salvaged but whether it will ever again be airworthy is questionable.

RAAF Point Cook Air Museum also received an ex-RNZAF Harvard as a static display item. (*Courtesy of RAAF Museum, Canberra ACT*)

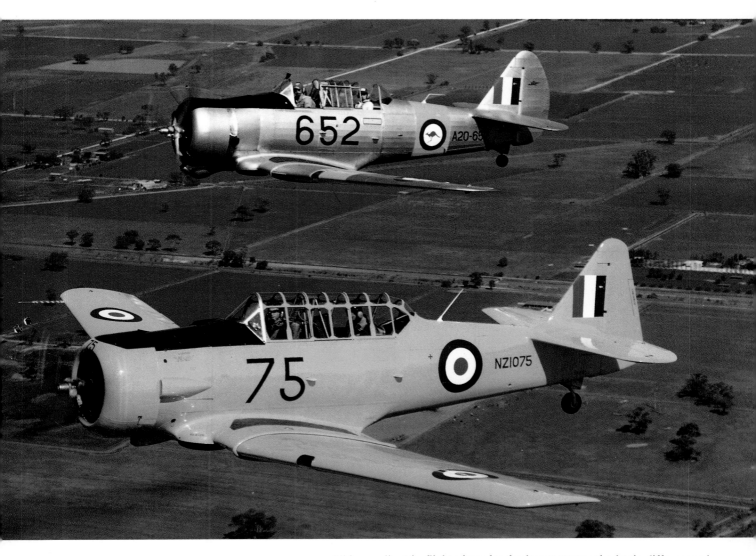

This excellent in-flight view clearly demonstrates the basic differences in appearance of the North American Harvard and the Commonwealth Wirraway.

The occasion was the Antique Aeroplane Association of Australia's annual 'Fly-In', which was held at Easter 1989.

The Harvard in the foreground (NZ1075) is owned by John Barnes of Melbourne and was flown on this occasion by Steve Chapman. The Wirraway in the background (A20-652) is owned and was flown by Stephen D. Eath, of Albury, New South Wales. (*Copyright, 1989, N.M. Parnell*)

Flyable Wirraways are something of a rarity nowadays. This is A20-653
(BF-F) in the original wartime operational colours of the SE Asia combat
zone of World War II coming in to land at the 'Fly-In' held at Air World,
Wingratta, Victoria. The date was 29 March 1986 and the pilot on that
occasion was Alan Searle. (*Courtesy N.M. Parnell*)

4 The Wirraway Story

The Wirraway CA1 General Purpose aircraft, was named from the Aboriginal word for Challenge, which was appropriate enough for it was the first aircraft to be built by the newly formed Commonwealth Aircraft Corporation Proprietary Limited of Port Melbourne, Victoria.

The origins of both the company and the concept can be traced back to an evaluation of the future role of the Royal Australian Air Force (RAAF) made by Marshal of the Royal Air Force Sir John Salmond as early as 1928, the Salmond Report. Lack of funding, public apathy and no obvious threat delayed any implementation of even the preliminary scheme for five squadrons for almost a decade. But with the Japanese invasion of China, Hitler's rise to power in Germany, Mussolini's bully-boy tactics in Ethiopia and other grave events, by the mid-1930s a different mood was beginning to appear in Australia as in the other democracies. Influencial Australian businessmen like Essington Lewis returned from Europe deeply concerned at Australia's vulnerability in this field.

It was a statement issued by the then Prime Minister of Australia, Archdale Parker, on 18 June 1936, when it was first becoming clear that the threat of war in Europe might leave Australia unable to rely on the traditional British guarantee for protection against Japanese expansion, that proved the final catalyst. Parker expressed the view, now common among his countrymen, that there existed a need for the Commonwealth to manufacture its own aircraft and aero-engines and be self-reliant in both respects. 'The development of such manufacture by Australian interests within the Commonwealth is regarded by the Government not only as essential to the defence of the Commonwealth, but in addition, a decided benefit to Australian industry.'

It was as a direct result of this statement that a mission was sent to Britain, Europe and the United States to examine and evaluate foreign designs that would be suitable for the initial production runs of the proposed new industry. The three men of this mission were Wing Commander Wackett and Squadron Leaders Harrison and Murphy, RAAF, and their brief was to select a relatively simple, modern and reliable aircraft with General Purpose (GP) abilities. The aircraft were to have all the most up-to-date features, variable-pitch propellers, low-wing form, stressed-skin, all-metal fuselage, and were to become the first forty such Australian-built aircraft. It was not high performance that they were seeking so much as a good, modern and easy-to-build type on which to establish the new industry.

Hitherto it had been a matter of routine, indeed patriotic faith, that British types were automatically selected and used by the RAAF. It is a measure of the Australians' growing independent spirit and hard-headed business sense that no such inhibitions influenced the mission on this occasion, for their final recommendations were for the adoption under licence of the North American NA-26 trainer. There were protests from some of the traditionalists in the Government at the acceptance of an American rather than British aircraft but these were very sensibly overruled.

Commonwealth Aircraft Company records provide a detailed description of how the Wirraway was constructed.

The mainplanes were of aluminium alloy construction employing a single spar with channel section spar caps and sheet metal webs. Both upper and lower spar caps were divided into sections, being spliced at each joint with a short length of similar section. The spar web was made of four sheets of aluminium alloy of varying thicknesses, which were joggled and lap jointed. Reinforcements and rib attach angles were riveted to the faces of the spar. Flanged type ribs extended from the spar to the trailing edge and forward of the spar to the leading edge. The former ribs were known as trailing edge ribs. The entire assembly was covered with aluminium alloy sheet reinforced with stringers.

Flanged intercostals supported ailerons and flaps along the trailing edge. The ribs were attached to spar and intercostals by means of formed angles. Access doors were provided on the lower surface to facilitate servicing. These could be used, if convenient, for access to the interior, for repairs. All ribs were pressed aluminium alloy sheet, with channel type flanges and pressed lightening holes. The trailing edge consisted of a formed section of aluminium alloy riveted to the upper skin covering and extended inboard from the aileron cut-out in each wing. Wing-tips of aluminium alloy consisted of two ribs, two intercostals, and top and bottom covering. Bolt angles, made from aluminium alloy extruded section, formed the medium by which the outer wing panels were bolted to the centre section.

The centre section of aluminium alloy construction throughout, incorporated riveted channel section spars and pressed channel-type ribs. Reinforcement and rib attach angles were riveted vertically across the faces of the spars. Machined aluminium alloy blocks were bolted inside the top spar caps to form the attach for the centre section to the fuselage. The covering was aluminium alloy sheet varying in thickness at different stations; the upper skin between the spars being reinforced by a corrugated section. The centre ribs were cut to give accommodation for the fuel tanks. Trailing edge ribs extended from the rear face of the rear spar.

The wheel housing assembly was riveted to the front face of the front spar. The lower surface of the centre section between the spars was made up of a removeable portion, known as the fuel tank cover, which was attached to each spar by means of anchor nuts located along the inside of the lower spar caps. When this cover was bolted into position it formed an integral part of the centre section construction. The major sub-assemblies of the complete wing assembly could be removed from the fuselage as one unit, or removed individually. Removal of the complete wing assembly or centre section could be accomplished with landing gear installed on centre section and locked in the extended position.

The landing flaps were of aluminium alloy construction throughout incorporating a 'hat' section spar and pressed channel ribs. A 'Z' section formed the leading edge, the trailing edge was a standard formed section. Flaps were secured to the wings by a continuous-type hinge. Actuating rods were attached to the flap spar by eyebolts which rotated in phosphor-bronze bearings. Dive bombing flaps, interconnected with the landing flaps and operated by the same hydraulic jack, were fitted to Mk. III aircraft, (Nos. A20-623 onward). These flaps opened upwards as the flaps moved downwards.

The ailerons' construction was similar to that of the flaps and incorporated a pressed channel type spar, flanged nose and trailing ribs and channel section trailing edge suitably reinforced by gussets. Cat aluminium alloy hinge brackets were provided. Covering forward of the spar was sheet metal, whilst fabric formed the covering for the trailing edge and also extended over the nose skin. Ailerons were fitted with three hinges. Each aileron incorporated a booster tab.

The fuselage frame consisted of the engine mount, the forward and aft sections of welded chrome-molybdenum steel tubing and steel fitting construction and the bottom section, aft of station number six, which was of aluminium alloy semi-monocoque construction. An auxiliary tail skid and jack pad were riveted to the aft end of this monocoque. An overturn structure was incorporated in the forward section of the fuselage frame, behind the front cockpit, for protection of the crew in event of a nose-over. The fire-wall was a single sheet of aluminium alloy, provided with reinforcing angles about its circumference.

Fuselage side panels were fabric-covered aluminium alloy frames readily detachable, being secured to the fuselage by screws. The two tandem cockpits were under one enclosure incorporating individual manually-operated sliding sections at each cockpit, for entry and exit. Both sections could be locked closed or in several intermediate positions. Seats were mounted on steel tubes and were adjustable to selective vertical positions. The rear seat was reversible, being pivoted on a bearing incorporated in the fuselage frame. Provisions were made for an instrument flying hood in the front cockpit of the Mk. I and II aircraft.

The landing gear was of a single leg, half-fork, fully cantilever design. Each unit consisted of a cylinder and piston, by means of which shock absorption through air and oil was provided. The piston and cylinder were interconnected by forged chrome-moly steel torsion links. A heat-treated steel fork was bolted to the lower end of the piston and carried the axle. This fork was heat treated to 160,000-180,000 psi. The gear was fully retractable inboard and forward of the wing centre section front spar. Hydraulic power was supplied normally by an engine-driven hydraulic pump and in the event of failure of that pump or its connections, by means of a hand operated pump. The landing gear was operated by double-acting rams, with mechanically operated spring-load latches and lockpins at the retracted and extended positions respectively. The gear could be lowered from either cockpit but as a safety catch was incorporated in the front cockpit quadrant, it could not be raised by rear cockpit controls.

Mechanical indicators and an electric warning horn were located in the front cockpit. Hydraulic wheel brakes were fitted. The tail-wheel assembly consisted of an aluminium (later magnesium) alloy wheel support casting attached to two fittings bolted to the rear end of the monocoque, a swivel post assembly and fork, mounted on roller bearings in the support casting and a pneudraulic shock strut. An eleven inch diameter wheel and tyre was mounted on the axle which was an integral part of the fork. The wheel was steerable and controlled by the rudder pedals and cables incorporated in the rudder control system. A tail-wheel locking device was also fitted. The tyre pressure was 60 psi. The hydraulically operated landing flaps were controlled in a manner similar to the retracting landing gear. A calibrated indicator, adjacent to the landing gear position indicator in the front cockpit, showed the position of the flaps from the UP position (0 degrees) to the DOWN position (60 degrees). The hand pump was used for emergency operation of the landing gear and flaps.

Of the Wirraway's tail unit, the rudder frame was of aluminium-alloy construction consisting essentially of a torque tube, pressed flanged ribs, channel trailing edge and metal covered leading edge were fabric covered. The elevators consisted of two interchangeable sections. The construction of the elevators followed the pattern of the rudder, including the fabric covering. The tailplane also comprised two interchangeable sections each of aluminium alloy construction and consisting of a front and rear spar, pressed flanged ribs, stiffening intercostals and metal covering. The fin was of aluminium alloy construction throughout, the assembly consisting of a front and rear spar, pressed flanged ribs, stiffening intercostals and metal covering. Trim tabs were fitted to the rudder and elevators.

With regard to the electrical system on the Wirraway, an engine-driven generator of voltage controlled type and control panel were fitted. A 12-volt battery was mounted on a shelf at the right hand side of the fire-wall, below the oil tank. All wiring, with the exception of H.T. wires, was of glazed cotton-braided type with metal terminal lugs pressed and soldered into place. Each wire was numbered or coded with a colour designation like the wiring diagram. Two 240-Watt landing lights were fitted to the aircraft and built in the leading edge of each wing. Navigation lights were built into wing-tips and fin; indentification lights being fitted in the rear fuselage. A heated Pitot static head was located on the starboard wing.

All the instrument panels were mounted on shock absorbers to prevent damage to the instruments due to engine vibration. A sub-panel was also fitted in the front cockpit below the main instrument panel and a small panel installed aft of the rear cockpit on the port side at the prone bombing position. The main panels were directly illuminated by lamps located behind a hinged reflector covering each panel. The following instruments were installed on the instrument panel in the front cockpit: air speed indicator; turn and bank indicator; rate of climb indicator; directional gyro; gyro horizon; altimeter; compass; clock; exhaust gas analyser; tachometer; manifold pressure gauge; engine gauge unit; and engine cylinder head temperature indicator. On the sub-panel were located, air temperature indicator; suction gauge; connections for camera; engine starter switch; bomb jettison switch. The rear cockpit panel had altimeter; air speed indicator; turn and bank indicator; clock; compass; tachometer. The bomb-aimer's panel contained an air speed indicator and altimeter, which were not fitted on later Mk.III Wirraways.

The fuel and oil tanks and hydraulic fluid reservoirs were manufactured from aluminium-alloy and were repairable by welding. The fuel tanks were covered with a rubber and canvas fire proofing medium but after aircraft No. A20-768, this protection was discontinued.

The Wirraway's armament comprised two forward-firing .303 inch Vickers machine-guns with synchronising gear plus a freely rotating Vickers G.O. No 1 which was carried on a hydraulically controlled hoist in the rear cockpit in the Mk I and II aircraft. The gun could move on a track in the form of a circular arc. Eight magazines, each holding sixty rounds were carried. A camera-gun could be mounted on the gun hoist, replacing the gun. Pyrotechnics included a Very pistol for signal flares, located on the right hand side of the front cockpit, stowage for eight cartridges being provided opposite.

On Mk I and II aircraft two forced-landing flares could be dropped through launching tubes in the rear fuselage; reconnaissance flares (when used) were carried on centre section mechanical bomb carriers and released by the bomb release mechanism and controls. Eighteen bomb slips were built into the aircraft; there were two universal carriers on each outer wing. Total normal bomb load was 500 lb, but for the overload case 1,000 lb could be carried. Light series carriers were located in the trailing edge portion of the centre section, just forward of the flaps. These carried practice bombs. A course-setting bomb-sight, Mk VII or IX, was fitted below the rear cockpit floor. Later aircraft, Mk IIIs from A20-623 onwards, had all-gun armament (including the camera gun) deleted and the aft end of the cockpit enclosed by a streamline steel-framed Perspex canopy. The radio transmitter and receiver were fitted in the rear cockpit, together with a trailing aerial and winch. The aerial had to extend 200 feet to be effective. Other equipment carried in this cockpit included a hand-operated carbon-tetrachloride fire-extinguisher, readily accessible from the ground as well as from the cockpit, by opening a hinged door. An F24 camera could be installed when it was not desired to use the prone bombing position.

The Wirraway's flying controls consisted of those operating the rudder, elevators, ailerons and trim tabs. Non-corrodible flexible steel cables were used. Smooth and effective control was assured by use of sealed type ball bearings at all pulleys, bellcranks and control-surface hinge points. These were packed with lubricant on assembly and required no further lubrication. A complete set of flying controls was installed in each cockpit, all controls being readily adjustable. A surface control lock was provided in the front cockpit. Engine controls comprised throttle, mixture and propeller control handles all assembled in a single quadrant located on the left side of each cockpit and interconnected by rods. Hot air from the exhaust manifold shroud could be taken into the carburettor through a valve in the air mixture chamber: this was controlled by a handle with notches providing vernier adjustment. The hand fuel pump handle was located on the left side of each cockpit, while fuel selector valve controls were adjacent. The engine starter push-button was located on the instrument sub-panel in the front cockpit. The engine switch was placed ahead of the rear cockpit on the left side. It was operated by mechanical linkage via a lever in the front left-hand corner of each cockpit, ahead of the throttle controls.

The Pratt & Whitney Wasp engine powered this aircraft, driving a *three-bladed*, controllable-speed, metal propeller. The engine was a nine-cylinder, single row R-1340 S1H1G radial, the first of many to be built under licence from Pratt & Whitney by the CAC

Engine Division. This engine was rated normally 550 hp at 5,000 feet at 2,200 rpm, take-off as 600 hp at 2,250 rpm. Thus maximum horsepower was 600 and the weight was 1,750 lb. Rate of climb was 1,950 feet per minute and endurance at operating speed was 3.07 hours. The range at operational speed at 450 hp was 640 miles, and at best economical speed was 850 miles. The engine could be turned with a hand starting crank which was stowed inside the fuselage side access door.

Maximum speed at crusing altitude (8,600 feet) was 220 mph; with 177 mph at sea-level, 199 mph at 9,000 feet and 209 mph at the critical altitude of 13,000 feet. The service ceiling was 23,000 feet. Landing speed at normal weight with flaps down was 65 mph, with flaps up, 70 mph.

Gross weight for the Wirraway was 5,575 lb normal, 6,450 lb maximum. Fuel capacity was ninety-two gallons total and reserve was sixteen gallons. Oil capacity was 8¾ gallons. The Wirraway's wing area was 256 square feet, span forty-three feet. Overall length came out at 27 feet 10 inches. Normal wing loading was 21.98 lb per square foot and power loading normal at 9.3 lb/hp.

The Wirraway at war. An Australian Commonwealth Wirraway conducts a very low-level sweep over the beaches at Port Douglas, North Queensland, on 17 March 1944. The occasion was the 6th Division's landing exercises conducted there during Exercise 'Douglas'.

Both Wirraways and Boomerangs of No. 5 Squadron, RAAF, were used to simulate Japanese opposing air strikes against the landing craft and invasion fleet during this operation, conducting mock strafing and bombing runs over the beach-heads. (*Courtesy of Australian War Memorial, Canberra. A.C.T.*)

Following the acceptance of Australian Mission's report a consortium of six of the leading Australian industrial companies formed the CAC with working capital of one million Australian pounds, on 17 October 1936. A factory was established the following April at Fishermen's Bend, Melbourne and work commenced. The Company's first aircraft were the two North American types which were used as received from North American Aviation, Inc. in mid-1937 and evaluated by the RAAF. They were assigned the RAAF numbers A20-1 and 2 respectively. Two versions were offered for selection. The first was the NA-32 (NA-16-1A), later the Yale, which featured a fixed undercarriage and a two-bladed propeller (Serial number 32-387). The second was the NA-33 (NA-16-2K) with the retractable gear and a three-bladed propeller (Serial number 32-388). Following their transfer to the RAAF on 2 February 1938, it was the latter that was finally chosen.

In June 1938 the Australian Government announced the awarding of a contract to CAC for the first forty Wirraways, (the construction of which had already been mooted the year before) with the firm intention to order another sixty or seventy later. This was despite a disparaging report by Marshal of the Air Force Sir Edward Ellington, who expressed reservations about the Wirraway's fitness for GP or light bombing duties, indeed for anything other

than air training. The Air Board stoutly defended their choice (and were to be proved right by events) while the Government assured the public that the price paid for the licence was 'satisfactory'.

In fact Kindelberger had struck a hard bargain for the licencing agreement. North American was paid an initial licence fee of one hundred thousand US dollars, royalties of thirty thousand US dollars for the specifications and manufacturing data plus a royalty of one thousand US dollars for each of the first batch of twenty-five aircraft produced. Furthermore, additional royalties of six hundred US dollars per aircraft were to be made on the next seventy-five machines before all payments ceased.

Various modifications, including fitment of twin, synchronized, forward-firing machine-guns in the upper forward fuselage firing through blast troughs, bomb gear and associated rear assembly strengthening for dive-bombing, camera and radio, were suggested and incorporated, and the name Wirraway assigned. The first of the series made its maiden flight, piloted by Flight Lieutenant H. Boss-Walker, RAAF, on 8 March 1939, as the Wirraway Mark I. In July 1939 the first three production Wirraways were accepted into service by the RAAF. (*Courtesy of Rockwell International Archives*)

Work underway on Wirraway aircraft. Total production was 755 machines built between March 1939 and June 1946. (*Courtesy Hawker de Havilland Archives, Melbourne*)

(left)
The success of the first experimental Wirraways resulted in further orders on the outbreak of war in September of that year and production was increased to forty-five aircraft a month in 1941. The Wirraway was never intended to be in any way a combat aircraft but circumstances dictated otherwise. However, from the start the Wirraway was built with an armament of two machine-guns and could carry underwing bombs. Thus when No. 21 squadron RAAF was sent to Malaya just prior to the Japanese invasion they were soon thrown into the turmoil of total war. Other Wirraway-equipped squadrons went to New Guinea where they fought gallantly against heavy odds. Others served in the south Pacific island campaigns in New Guinea and onward as target spotters, dive- bombers, supply and transport aircraft and observation machines. The Australian Wirraways were by far and away the most combat-used version of the T-6 during World War II and we will return to some of their outstanding actions in a later chapter.

In addition to their impressive battle record, the chief role of the Australian Wirraway remained, as with their American, Canadian and British bretheren, that intended for them, advanced training aircraft. Wirraways were the mainstay of the Empire Air Training Scheme (EATS) in Australia and it was largely due to the enterprise of CAC that this scheme was carried out so completely and that it was able to accomplish the training of many thousands of young Australian pilots and aircrew who later served the world over. Here a stepped echelon formation of Wirraways with yellow engine cowlings is seen on a training flight during 1943.

The original Wirraway programme was for 620 machines and this was completed by June 1942, but a further programme for additional aircraft of this type increased the grand total constructed to 755. As with the Texan and Harvard, however, the story of the Wirraway was far from finished with the arrival of VJ day! (*Department of Public Records, Canberra ACT*)

(above)
One of the very early Commonwealth Wirraways (A20-21) is seen to good advantage in this air-to-air photograph. The aircraft's armament is clearly displayed with the two forward-firing .303-inch Vickers machine-guns with synchronising gear plus a freely rotating Vickers G.O. No 1 which was carried on a hydraulically controlled hoist in the rear cockpit in the Mk I and II aircraft. The gun could move on a track in the form of a circular arc. Eight magazines each holding sixty rounds were carried. Alternately a camera gun could be mounted on the gun hoist, replacing the gun. Pyrotechnics included a Very pistol for signal flares, located on the right-hand side of the front cockpit, stowage for eight cartridges being provided opposite.

On Mk I and II aircraft two forced-landing flares could be dropped through launching tubes in the rear fuselage; reconnaissance flares (when used) were carried on centre section mechanical bomb carriers and released by the bomb release mechanism and controls. Eighteen bomb slips were built into the aircraft; there were two universal carriers on each outer wing. Total normal bomb load was 500 lb, but for the overload case 1,000 lb could be carried. Light series carriers were located in the trailing edge portion of the centre section, just forward of the flaps. These carried practice bombs. A course setting bomb-sight, Mk VII or IX, was fitted below the rear cockpit floor. Later aircraft, Mk IIIs from A20-623 onward, had all-gun armament, (including the camera gun) deleted and the aft end of the cockpit enclosed by a streamlined steel-framed Perspex canopy. The radio transmitter and receiver were fitted in the rear cockpit, together with a trailing aerial and winch. The aerial had to extend 200 feet to be effective. (*Courtesy Department of Public Records, Canberra ACT*)

A fine aerial study of Commonwealth Wirraway 142 of the Royal Australian Air Force on a training mission.

There were several variants to the standard Wirraway design, both completed and proposed. The Mark I was a GP design which had the CAC contract number CA1. They were allocated the serial numbers 1 to 40 and took RAAF numbers A20-3-42 (Mk I). Further batches of GP Wirraways followed, the Mark II, (contract CA3) taking serial numbers 41-100 and RAAF numbers A-20-43-102 (Mk.II); CA5, serials 103-134 and RAAF numbers A-20-103-134 (Mk.II); CA7, serial numbers 135-234 and RAAF serials 135-234 (Mk.II). A combined GP/Trainer variant followed under contract CA8, with serial numbers 436 to 635, and RAAF numbers A-20-235-434 (Mk.II) and this was followed by a dive-bomber variant under contract CA9 with serial numbers 636-823, RAAF numbers A-20-435 to 622 (Mk.II). A further GP batch under contracts CA10 and CA10A were later cancelled, but another dive-bomber group went ahead under contract CA16, with serial numbers 1075 to 1224 and RAAF numbers A-20-623-722 (Mk.III). Finally under contract CA20 another dive-bomber batch was proposed for conversion for RAN use but subsequently cancelled. Total production was therefore 755 between March 1939 and June 1946.

They were all two-seat, low-wing monoplanes. The Wirraway had a welded steel tube fuselage and wings of stressed-skin construction. The tail unit was metal with fabric covered control surfaces. (*Courtesy Department of Public Records, Canberra ACT*)

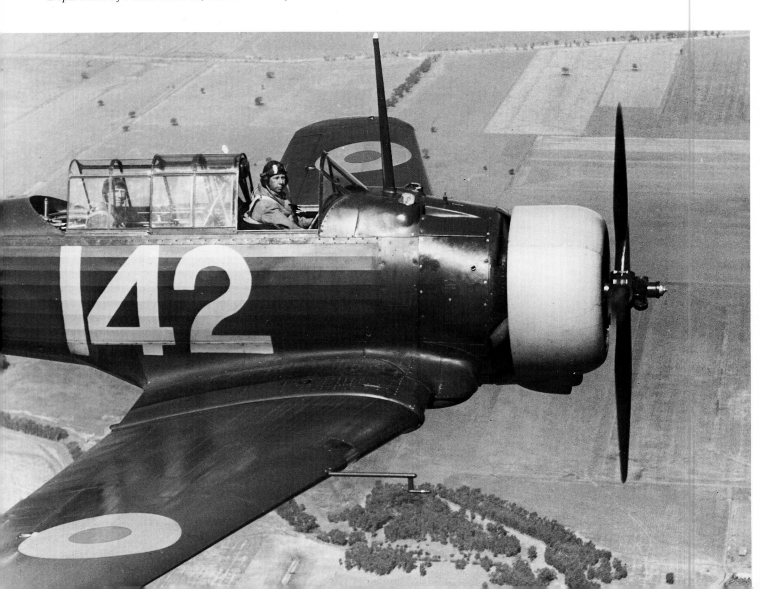

Another variant from the T-6 stable was the Australian Commonwealth Boomerang single-seater fighter. This was developed from the NA-16 from the NA-33 Wirraway built under licence. The Royal Australian Air Force designated it as the A-46 and, as such, it was the only Australian home-produced fighter-bomber built during World War II. Born as a direct result of the crisis situation of 1941-42 and the need for fighter aircraft CAC utilised the Pratt & Whitney 14-cylinder Twin Wasp engine. To speed production the Boomerang line utilised an adaptation of the Wirraway cockpit with a fairing, as well as the now reinforced centre section, undercarriage, tail assembly and other components, all built directly from Wirraway drawings. Although it looked similar to the American P-64 fighter, North American had absolutely no design input into the Boomerang itself.

This is A46-128 in flight and showing to good advantage the 'spined' engine exhaust, gunsight and one of the two 20-mm cannon, which, along with four Browning machine-guns, formed the Boomerang's armament. (*Copyright Trethewey, Oppem, Belgium*)

The Wirraway at war. Mareeba, North Queensland, Australia, 8 May 1944. Boxes containing field operations rations are being fitted underneath the mainplanes of a Wirraway of No. 5 Squadron, Royal Australian Air Force. These boxes of rations were dropped to the troops of the 17th Infantry Brigade during a combined supply dropping exercise.

The RAAF's Wirraways were frequently used in this role during the campaigns in New Guinea and Burma and proved invaluable in keeping the forward troops supplied in thick jungle territories.

In the background is the fighter derivative of the Wirraway, the Commonwealth Boomerang (A46-192) with the white tail and rear fuselage markings common to the S.E. Asia Theatre of Operations. (*Courtesy of Australian War Memorial, Canberra. A.C.T.*)

(*right*)

The most celebrated combat of the war involving a Commonwealth Wirraway was probably that which took place on 26 December 1942, over Gona, New Guinea. Pilot Officer Jack Archer was on routine reconnaissance patrol over the famous wreck in the harbour there in Wirraway A20-103 ('Chuff-Chuff') in company with another Wirraway. Fortunately this aircraft, as well as being used for dive-bombing operations at the time with universal bomb carriers under the wings, was also fitted with two forward-firing machine-guns.

Another aircraft was spotted by Archer's observer, Sergeant J.L. Coulston, some 1,000 feet below them. At first it was taken for a friendly but then Coulston yelled a warning over the intercom. 'Hell, it's a . . . Zero'. And so it was, a Japanese Navy Mitsubishi A6M Reisen 'Zeke' or 'Zero' fighter, considerably faster, more powerfully armed and more manoeuvrable than the Wirraway, or indeed most contemporary Allied fighter planes!

It was a time for quick action and Archer did the only thing possible to prevent the destruction of two Australian machines, he attacked!

As he dived towards the enemy, which fortunately had still not spotted them, Archer pressed the firing button at 200 yards range and kept his finger firmly on the trigger until within fifty feet of the Japanese machine. To his intense relief as he pulled his Wirraway in a tight turn, Archer saw the Zero fall flaming into the sea.

Coulston, later said that Archer had done the only possible thing when he attacked. Had he missed things would have turned out very differently for them all. Asked how it felt to attack a Zero in a Wirraway, Archer replied he couldn't say, 'I didn't have time to think about it. I was lucky to get in the first burst. It was certainly good to see him crash into the sea.' He was duly rewarded with a crate of beer on his return to base!

Post-war after many adventures, Archer's mount was eventually salvaged and restored and is now on display at the Australian War Memorial. (*Courtesy Australian War Memorial, Canberra ACT*).

Another unique event. The last-ever Commonwealth Wirraway to fly on active service with the Royal Australian Air Force is pictured here making her farewell flight over Sydney Harbour Bridge. Very few survive today but in recent years some worthwhile efforts have been made to preserve some, even if few of them are flyable.

The story of Archers' A20-103 Wirraway is the most well-known of these few survivors. After being passed on to another pilot in his unit for a time, this machine was returned to Australia for a refit and refurbishment. Archers' personal 'Chuff Chuff' emblem, a wheeled Chinese Dragon, his red and white 'Rising Sun' kill marking and three yellow bombing mission registers, were painted over and replaced by the Squadron Crest. All the aircraft's armament was removed at the same time and the Wirraway was operated by No. 3 Communications Unit for a while. Then it went to No. 7 Aircraft Depot for storage. It survived many years of neglect and today has been fully restored and is a static display at the Australian War Memorial in Canberra, A.C.T. (*Courtesy Hawker de Havilland, Melbourne*)

5 Exports and Offspins

The T-6 was one of the most successful aircraft designs of all times. Its arrival filled an urgently-felt need in the air forces of not just the major powers like the United States, Great Britain, France, Canada and Australia, but a whole host of lesser nations that wished to modernise their air fleets under the impetus of World War II. The Texan was the right aircraft at the right time in more ways than one! But before we examine in detail the enormous diversity of customers for the T-6 and the variety of uses that they put this little aircraft to, let us take a look at the final conventional developments of the type by North American in the closing stages of the war, along with a few experimental and 'oddball' customisations of the basic airframes that took place during this same period.

The story of the Ranger-engined Texan is a complex one. The Fairchild Caminez Engine Corporation was set up as a subsidiary of the Fairchild Aviation Corporation in 1925, becoming just the plain Fairchild Engine Corporation four years later. When, during the same period, the noted engine designer Walter F. Davis came up with an in-line, air-cooled inverted cylinder aero-engine at Wright Aeronautical it found no favour there. Seeking a more successful engine to market than his own failed four-cylinder, four-stroke, Caminez cam-drive disaster, the head of the Long Island company, Sherman Fairchild, took Davis and his engine onboard immediately.

The original six-cylinder Ranger 6-390 in-line engine was progressively developed through to the Model 770, a 290 hp, 12-cylinder inverted engine which had rows of cylinders in a 60-degree 'V' form. Uprated steadily through to a 575 hp model, the Ranger in-lines found some limited use with Fairchild training aircraft but no large contracts, and even after the outbreak of war in Europe its projected use in the Navy's Curtiss SO3C-1 never materialised and the reputation of the engine itself suffered unfairly accordingly. A similar fate befell the projected Bell Aircraft Corporation's XP-77, a wood-construction, high-speed fighter, which was also cancelled.

It was then that Fairchilds proposed the marriage of the upgraded 770 in-line engine with North American's outstandingly successful trainer in order to provide both a market for their engines and also the Army Air Force with a training aircraft that more reflected the type of aircraft their new young fighter pilots would be flying in combat.

The T-6 is famous for its radial engine, both because of its distinctive sound and for its readily identifiable shape. The United States Navy had always favoured radial-engine aircraft from the 1930's onward, but the USAAF was less enamoured, and, other than for fighters like the Republic P-47 Thunderbolt, it was the inline-engined fighters like the Curtiss P-39 and P-40 Kittyhawks and Warhawks and North American P-51 Mustang that predominated. This fact was coupled with the fear that huge demand for the Pratt & Whitney Wasp engine might result in shortages and bottlenecks in production, and helped turned the USAAF's attentions to Fairchild's suggestions on the possibilities of developing an inline-engined version of the T-6 for their future air training needs.

It was not a success and only one prototype was ever built. Fairchilds, the engine manufacturers, had lost their last gamble and went to the wall. The reasons for the rejection, despite the very impressive figures achieved, are these. First-and-foremost, like the anticipated aluminium shortage earlier, the feared shortage of Pratt & Whitney engines never materialised. Reliability and continuity of production far outweighed the height and speed advantages of the XAT-6E which after all was a *trainer* and not competing as a fighter with the AT-6D. It did not need either of the former's desirable assets to continue to churn out thousands of young pilots year-after-year!

Secondly was the unreliability and temperament of the Ranger engine itself. Noisy it might be, rough-and-ready also, maybe, but the good 'ole P & W kept flying steadily on and required but minimum care and maintenance to keep it that way. The in-line was smaller, had to work harder for the same effect and thus suffered from gross over-heating. Although Fairchilds' engineers desperately tried to overcome these problems by the fitting of sheet metal baffles between each cylinder, and also invented a chemical bond heat-dissipating fin to each cylinder barrel, the *Al-Fin* process, they could not save the day. Thirdly, by the time the trials were over the end of the war was clearly in sight. There were thousands of surplus Texans all over the free-world, jet fighters were already in the skies and money was getting tight again as Governments started to cut back on funding. The XAT-6E was doomed before it even flew; but it was a nice try.

One final word on this aircraft is required. It is a fact that North American official records show only a single XAT-6E conversion. It is also a documented and photographically-proven fact that *two* such machines competed against each other in post-war civil air races. How can these two facts be squared?

The original North American/Fairchild conversion was bought privately and registered as NX7410. Piloted by Margaret McGrath it became the top qualifier for the 1947 female competition, the Halle Trophy Race, held at the National Air Races at Cleveland, Ohio, logging 223.325 mph and was said to have exceeded 240 mph. However, the old engine unreliability let it down again and she later had to withdraw.

The other 'XAT' was a conventional T-6 bought and converted privately by Dori Marland. It carried civilian registration N61268. It carried at various periods of its brief life the names 'Wingwax' and 'Spray Wax', large numerals '49' on its main fuselage and the 'Sohio' sponsorship logo on the streamlined fairing abaft the cockpit. This particular machine crashed during the self-same 1947 Halle Trophy Race.

The AT-6F/SNJ-6 was the final war production model of the Texan. These were AT-6Ds taken from the existing NA-121 contract and modified. The most obvious external change was the fitting of an integral, one-piece moulded Plexiglas (Perspex) rear canopy section in place of the previous ribbed movable section. This was made possible due to the complete dropping of the all machine-gun and bomb-carrying potential from the model. Complementary to this the rear seat was no longer required to swivel and was made a forward-facing fixture. The wing and nose machine-guns were also deleted, as were the underwing racks for light bombs. In place of the latter came an under the centreline fuselage fixture for mounting a twenty-gallon drop tank for extra fuel bunkerage. It was positioned just abaft the wheel wells.

Another identifying feature of this Mark of Texan was the fitting of a large propeller-spinner to complete the aerodynamic clean-up of the aircraft. Not obvious was the fact that the outer wing panels were strengthened on this model. The original US Army Air Force order was for 1,375 of these aircraft, but these included the Navy orders which, in common with earlier dashes, were procured on Army Air Force contracts. From this total 417 were cancelled at the end of the war and the Navy took delivery of 931. Of the twenty-five that were completed as AT-6Fs these were mainly assigned to Army Air Force Reserve units. None of these aircraft were transferred to the RAF or related air forces, so consequently there was no Harvard equivalent of the AT-6F.

So much for the conventional development of the Texan. Apart from the metric-metered T-6s sold to France before her defeat in 1940, the American and Canadian-built Harvards and the Australian-built Wirraways, T-6s (or their derivatives) equipped numerous other air forces' inventories by 1945. And not just those of Allied nations!

Apart from the 111 aircraft actually supplied from the 230 French *Armée de l'Air* batch of

NA-57s of 5 September 1939, which fell intact into German hands in June 1940, and which were given Swastikas and *Balkenkreuz* and then pressed into *Luftwaffe* service, North American scored a more obvious 'own-goal' by supplying two of their early trainers (and consequently the wherewithall to construct good imitations of them), to the Japanese enemy.

These aircraft were not Texans but of the fixed-fuselage Yale types, a NA-16-4R with a 450 hp Pratt & Whitney R-985-8CG engine and a three-bladed propeller, the first arrived in Japan in September 1937. Later a NA-47 (NA-16-RW) was delivered in December of the same year and again was a one-off built for Japan that was identical to the BT-9 except for the fact that it was fitted with a larger engine, the Wright R-975-E3 and a two-bladed propeller. This machine (47-699), along with full manufacturing rights, was sold outright to Mitsubishi Heavy Industries and shipped disassembled to them at Yokohama on 16 December 1937. These aircraft were evaluated by the Japanese Navy as the KXA1 and KXA2 respectively as Navy Experimental Type A Trainers. The Japanese Navy found them good enough to imitate and the licence and manufacturing rights were purchased through an intermediary trading company. As the NA-16-4R and many modifications, chief of which was the fitting of a Nakajima 600 hp Kotobuki 2 Kai air-cooled radial engine, this Japanese version was built by K.K. Watanabe Tekkosho, who had the prototype flying by 1941. The Japanese aircraft also featured enlarged vertical tail surfaces. A batch of twenty-five more Navy Type 2 Intermediate Trainers followed up to November 1942, as the K1OW1.

Further Japanese production runs were carried out by the Nippon Hikoki KK, and, as the K5Y1, they built 150 of them between February 1943 and March 1944. Armament was a single, forward-firing 7.7 mm Type 97 machine-gun and maximum speed was 152 knots. In the Pacific War this American-styled trainer was allocated the usual Allied code names, which for trainers were trees. So, to the Texan, the Harvard, the T-Bird, the Wirraway and the many other names by which the T-6 flew, another can be added, the Oak.

Two special one-offs were built at Inglewood for overseas customers pre-war. The first was produced for Canada as the BC-1 (NA-36, 26-202) and was similar to the BT-9 except that it featured fully retractable landing-gear and had an armament of two. 30 machine-guns. Power plant was the larger Pratt & Whitney R-B40 engine. The order was dated 20 October 1936 and the purpose of the machine was for use as a demonstration aircraft for the basic trainer.

In Europe another such 'customer' was found in the form of the Dutch aircraft manufacturer Fokker Aircraft, who purchased a one-off NA-27 as its demonstration machine of a basic trainer for the European market. They ordered from the Inglewood plant on 1 December 1936 and took delivery of this machine (NA-16-2H, 27-312) which was similar to the NA-26, on 15 April 1937.

Also, in Scandinavia, the Royal Swedish Air Force, the *Flygvapnet*, on 2 August 1937 took delivery of one NA-16-4M, (31-386) which was similar to the BT-9 but with a different engine, the Wright R-975-E3 driving a two-bladed propeller. This machine was fitted with the broad Goodyear Airwheels to take into account soggy conditions on Lapland strips. The *Flygvapnet* also bought the airplane and manufacturing rights. The Swedes received a second machine of the same type (identical to the NA-31) on 28 September of the same year (38-540) which was shipped unassembled as part of the manufacturing agreement.

Once evaluated an initial order for thirty-five machines resulted in July 1938, the Swedish designation being SK 14. These had started to enter service by the following May. SAAB received two contracts, for eighteen and for twenty-three of these machines which were delivered during the war. Subsequent orders for Texans were to result from their experience with the Yale, and Sweden later purchased direct a total of 263 later models, which comprised 145 AT-16s (Swedish designation being SK16A), 112 T-6s (the SK16B) and six SNJ-2s (the SK16C).

On 10 January 1944, the US Army procured eighty-one AT-6Ds (NA-119) under Lend-

Lease for the Brazilian Air Force. Of this total, sixty-one were shipped south as completely-assembled airframe kits for final assembly on-site; ten as complete airframe sub-assemblies and the final ten as complete airframe partially sub-assembled in Texas. No US Army serials were allocated to these aircraft.

Reverting again to strictly Lend-Lease procurements, on 2 December 1941 the Bolivian Air Force, the *Cuerpo de Aviadores Boliviano*, was the recipient of three North American AT-6A-NTs and these were the sole representatives of this dash to reach South America under the agreement. One of these machines was actually for use by the US Army Air Corps mission in that country, although it was nominally charged against Bolivia's account.

During 1942 there was a vast increase in deliveries, and for Brazil, the *Aviacao Exercito do Brasil* (fourteen AT-6B-NTs in April), Chile, the *Fuerza Aerea Nacional de Chile* (fifteen AT-6B-NTs in April), Columbia, the *Fuerza Aerea Colombiana* (four AT-6B-NTs in April), Ecuador, the *Fuerza Aerea Ecuatoriana* (four AT-6B-NTs in April), Mexico, the *Fuerza Aerea Mexicana* (six AT-6B-NTs in June), Peru, the *Cuerpo de Aeronautica del Peru*, (nine AT-6B-NTs in April) Uruguay, the *Aeronautica Militar Uruguaya* (four AT-6B-NTs in February) and Venezuela, the *Servicio Aereo Militar Venezolana* (four AT-6B-NTs in March) received between them a total of sixty AT-6Bs.

Dan Hagedorn described their reception thus:

> 'These aircraft were intended as morale boosters and a statement of intention to honour obligations, and they achieved these purposes marvelously. Besides propaganda value, the AT-6B variant offered at least limited defensive and offensive capabilities as well, and proved ideally suited to Latin American conditions at practically every turn. It is not surprising that, of all types sent to the theater, Texans were the most numerous (483) . . . T-6s supplied under Lend-Lease and other US air programmes to follow (not to mention quantities purchased surplus) soon became the most common aircraft in military colours in South America.'

In 1943 this trickle became a flood which eventually totalled 545 Texans making them easily the most numerous US aircraft sent to South American air forces. Bolivia received nine AT-6C-10-NTs and fifteen AT-6D-NTs; Brazil twenty AT-6C-NTs, five AT-6C-5-NTs, ten AT-6C-10-NTs, thirty-five AT-6C-15-NTs, twenty-five AT-6D-NTs and twenty AT-6D-1-NTs, five AT-6C-15-NTs, ten AT-6C-15-NTs, and thirty-two AT-6D-NTs (one of which was lost in transit); Columbia, two AT-6C-NTs, two AT-6C-10-NTs, four AT-6C-15-NTs, thirty-eight AT-6D-NTs and six AT-6D-1-NTs; Ecuador three AT-6C-NTs, three AT-6C-15-NTs and six AT-6D-1-NTs; Guatamala, the *Cuerpo de Aeronautica Militar Guatemalteca*, three AT-6C-15-NTs; Haiti, the *Corps D'Aviation D'Haiti*, two AT-6C-15-NTs; Mexico thirty-one AT-6C-NTs, six AT-6C-5-NTs, twelve AT-6C-10-NTs, ten AT-6D-NTs, and twenty AT-6D-1-NTs; Nicaragua, the *Fuerza Aerea de la Guardia Nacional de Nicaragua*, three AT-6C-15-NTs; Paraguay, the *Fuerza Aerea Nacional del Paraguay*, three AT-6C-NTs; Peru twenty-five AT-6D-NTs; Salvador, the *Aviacion Militar Salvadorena*, three AT-6C-NTs and three AT-6D-1-NTs; Uruguay six AT-6D-1-NTs; and Venezuela five AT-6C-5-NTs, three AT-6C-15-NTs and five AT-6D-NTs.

In all, 192 T-6Cs and 219 T-6Ds were sent while ten AT-6F-NTs were supplied to Cuba, the *Cuerpo Aerea Ejercito de Cuba*, in addition to six AT-6C-NTs and three AT-6C-10-NTs.

Other Allied governments were in ready receipt of the Texan also, including the China and the Netherlands government in exile, and the Soviet Union which had eighty-four AT-6Cs assigned to them, of which eighty-two were delivered. Thirty of these trainers were shipped by way of the Arctic convoys to Archangel, the other fifty-four were handed over in Alaska in 1945, for transit through Siberia (the Alsib ferry route). But they returned none of them!

Finally, among the many variations on the basic T-6 theme were some single-seater fighter adaptations that deserve mention. The first of these was the NA-50A. This aircraft was a direct development from the NA-16 and seven were contracted by the Peruvian Air Force on 9 February 1939 as the NA-50 (50-948 to 50-954). North American chopped five feet from the overall wingspan of the AT-6 and one foot from the fuselage length. The reduced canopy was faired over to the rear with the radio stack shifted aft. An Aldis gunsight tube was fitted forward of the pilot's cockpit. The old-style BC-1 type rudder and fin shape was retained with a fixed tailwheel but the main undercarriage was fully retractable.

To give the new aircraft fighter credibility an 870 hp Wright R-1820-77 engine was fitted which drove a three-bladed propeller. This combination gave it a trial speed of 295 mph and a service ceiling of 32,000 feet. The Peruvian batch were fitted out as fighter-bombers and thus were armed with both guns and bombs. These guns were four Colt-Browning .30 calibre weapons, carried one in each wing and two more, fully synchronised, mounted in the actual engine cowling itself. Light racks under each wing gave it a bomb-carrying capacity of 550lb. Range unladen was 645 miles.

The NA-50A had its first flight on 1 September 1940 and all seven fighters were delivered to Peru by early 1941.

Following their own inspection and air testing of the first NA-50A in September 1939, the Siamese government (now Thailand), to whose original specification it had been designed, ordered six of these fighter aircraft on the following 30 November. They asked for some modifications, mainly to the armament which was upgraded to match European War standards where the need for a heavier punch was manifest. As well as the two 8-mm machine-guns in the wings and two more in the engine cowling, the Siamese fighter had two single 20-mm cannon slung in underwing fairings under each wing outboard the machine gun station. Being delivered later they incorporated the distinctive T-6 angular tailplane and rudder configuration, and had no Aldis sighting tube emplaced. Except for an improved landing gear equipment they were in all other respects identical to their Peruvian cousins and were completed and shipped out of Los Angeles harbour as the NA-68 (NA-50A, 68-3058 to 68-3063) in 1940.

These aircraft were destined never to reach Siam. While still at Hawaii, Vichy-France and Siam fought a brief and vicious little war that is now all but forgotten. Under the strict terms of the Neutrality Act the United States was loath to assist either side (one an ally of Nazi Germany the other flirting with Japan) and so the state Department acted swiftly and revoked their export licences.

The six fighters were returned to the States and taken into the USAAC inventory at Luke AAFB as 'fighter-trainers'. They were assigned the standard designation of P-64 and used by Training Command throughout the war. Five were scrapped but one survived to be sold privately and later became one of the exhibits of the Experimental Aircraft Association at Oshkosh in Wisconsin, a very unique relic indeed!

Yet a third single-seater fighter was developed from the basic NA design, this time in Australia where the CAC came up with the Boomerang concept. Early in 1942 the Japanese were sweeping all before them in their drive to conquer their 'Co-prosperity Sphere'. Hong Kong, the Philippines, Borneo, Malaya, Singapore, the Dutch East Indies, New Britain, Burma and New Guinea, all fell like a house of cards before them. The position of Australia looked very precarious indeed and the Japanese Zero fighters had met no serious aerial opposition while cutting their swathe of victories through the Pacific. Certainly these fast and agile fighters completely outclassed anything Australia could pit against them at this time and there was little prospect of either the British or the Americans being able to supply many in the foreseeable future.

A locally-constructed, highly manoeuvrable and hard-hitting interceptor was desperately needed. The people to quickly produce such a home-produced fighter seemed obvious and the manager of the Commonwealth Aircraft Corporation, Wing Commander Lawrence

Wackett, put his design team to work at once. The Australian Government gave design approval as early as 21 December 1941, and, on 2 February 1942, the initial contract for 105 machines was placed before a single machine had been built!

The idea that they evolved was for a small fighter using the most powerful engine then readily available to them (the 1,200 hp Pratt & Whitney R-1830-S34C-G 14-cylinder Twin Wasp radial then in local production for the twin-engined Beaufort torpedo-bomber) and around it to construct the machine. To save on man-hours as the need was urgent, the use of existing tooling and as many CAC Wirraway components as was possible was made integral to the design. Thus the Boomerang had centre section, undercarriage and tail unit almost identical to the Wirraway.

The fuselage structure was of steel tube with a wooden monocoque fairing extending from the cockpit to the rudder. A seventy gallon bullet-proof fuel tank was fitted in the fuselage, behind the pilot and two forty-five gallon tanks of moulded wood construction were located in the centre section. Increased range was afforded by a seventy gallon drop-tank. This gave a range of 1,600 miles. After the 106th aircraft, the pilot's seat and wing-tips were also constructed of moulded wood. The cockpit was amply protected with armour plating behind the pilot and a bullet proof windscreen was fitted. The armament consisted of two 20mm Hispano cannon and four .303 Browning machine-guns mounted in the wing. There were also underwing bomb racks. The wings, fin and tail were all-metal stressed skin construction, the control surfaces being fabric covered. The Boomerang was fitted with a three-bladed de Havilland propeller.

The first CA.12 Boomerang, made its debut flight from Fisherman's Bend on 29 May 1942, flown by test pilot Ken Fruin, just fourteen weeks after the rough drafts had been approved. The only major modifications required after tests were to the oil cooling system. A spinner was added to the propeller as well. 105 ordered off the drawing board and by September a steady flow was joining the RAAF. The wingspan was 36 feet, total wing area being 225 square feet. The length was 25 ft 6 inches and height was 11 feet 6 inches. All-up weight of this little fighter was 8,032 lb and its maximum speed was 305 mph at 15,000 feet. It had an outstanding climb rate claimed to be 2,940 ft./min which was better than the Spitfire I, Focke-Wulf 190 F-3 and the Curtiss P-40N Warhawk, and a service ceiling of 36,000 feet.

Since the Twin Wasp was a medium supercharged engine giving its greatest power with the high-speed blower at about 15,000 feet, this gave a limitation to the aircraft's performance. To overcome this a Boomerang was converted to take an improved supercharger. This aircraft became CA.14 and its performance was considerably higher than that of the CA.12. Further improvements were made including the fitment of sliding gills and an engine cooling fan. The intercooler air scoop on the port side of the CA.14 was deleted, the air being directed from the engine bay. A square fin and rudder replaced the conventional Boomerang type and this greatly modified aeroplane became the CA.14A.

However, at about this time, American high-altitude fighters were being landed and assembled in Australia, so that further work on the CA.14A was dropped. In total, 250 Boomerangs, including the CA.14A, were built. The various batches of CAC Boomerang fighters can be summarised thus: Contract CA12, Fighter Interceptor, Serial numbers 824 to 928, RAAF numbers A46-1-105; Contract CA13, Fighter Interceptor, Serial numbers 929 to 1023, RAAF numbers A46-106-200; Contract CA14, Fighter (with supercharger), 1073, RAAF Serial number 1001; CA14A, Fighter with supercharger, square fin and rudder, 1073, 1001; CA19, Fighter, Serial numbers 1024 to 1072; RAAF Serial numbers A46-201-249.

In America the US Navy's SNJ-5Cs modified for carrier landing training with navigation tables and tailhooks had continued in service working from the training carriers (TCVs) one of which was the USS *Sable* (IX. 81, formerly the mercantile *Greater Buffalo*).

These two photographs were taken in May 1945 aboard the *Sable*. The second view shows the Texan of Captain Schoech, USN, touching down on the flight-deck a little later. In the background a Grumman Wildcat fighter awaits its turn to follow suit. (*US National Archives, Washington, DC*)

Here a SNJ can be seen taking-off from the flight-deck (note the raised arrester-hook just in front of the rear wheel) while in the background another circles the carrier awaiting the chance to land back on again (notice the extended arrester-hook of the distant machine). (*US National Archives, Washington DC*)

Post-war, the T-6 continued to give good service in training aircrew for the building-up of brand-new air forces from those of former enemies and Allies who now found themselves in the new Alliance, that of the Anti-Communist Free World. Having spent six years destroying the air arms of Germany and Japan, both the United States and Great Britain now had to allocate resources to re-equipping these nations and the North American trainer played a great part in this.

Here is shown the very first North American T-6G trainer (2861-29) to be painted with the Rising Sun emblem of the Japanese Air-Self Defense Force which was turned over from a United States Air Force unit at Camp Matsushima, in the Miyagi Prefecture in 1954. Note the tail markings incorrectly show this as a 'JS Air Force' machine. (*Courtesy of Tadashi Nozawa*)

90

West Germany received large batches of T-6s and Harvards. On 1 July 1955 the *Bundeswehr* ordered 135 Harvard Mark IVs under the MDAP programme in order to set up the Temporary Flying Training Command. The 7.351 Flying Training Wing established at Landsberg first flew these aircraft and was followed, on 24 September 1956, by further imports of T-6J-CCFs from North America. With the *Flugdienststaffel* (FFS) these machines served faithfully and well, undergoing several minor modifications, until the early 1960s. A few served with WaSLw 30 (the Operational Training School for the F-84F fighters). Yet another T-6 nickname could be added to the seemingly endless list for the chrome-yellow coloured unarmed FFS training machines were dubbed 'Zitronenbombers' (Lemon bombers) by the instructors and novice pilots.

In addition to training some Harvards served as target tugs for radar-controlled flight-controller training with F1Kdo TSLw 1 at Kaufbeuren from 1964 onward. The FFS 'A's aerobatic team flew their Harvard IVs from Landsberg for many years. The final West German Harvard flight took to the air on 30 January 1962 with the machines flown by *Oberleutnant* Garske, *Leutnant* Kruger, *Leutnant* Stehli and SU Rohl. A final farewell ceremony was held at Kaufbeuren in the summer of 1964 when a check-nosed Harvard IV, suitably bedecked with black mourning crêpe ribbon from both wingtips, was officially 'discharged' from the service. (*German Federal Government Photograph Archive, Bonn*)

Three Dutch Harvards outside the Fokker factory for refurbishing after their hand-over from the Royal Air Force. Nearest the camera is FS737, which, on being handed over in September 1946, had seen no previous service with her original owners at all. FT148, beyond her, was handed over in August 1947, and similarly had not been flown before entering Dutch service.

A further forty ex-RCAF Harvards were delivered to the Netherlands East Indies in August 1948, two of which were damaged in transit. They were flown as trainers at the flying schools at Kalidjati. Those that survived were handed over to the Indonesian Republic in 1950 on independence. (*Courtesy Arthur Pearcy Archives*)

The Turkish Air Force received a grand total of 196 T-6/Harvard aircraft. The first batch of one hundred machines, AT-6Cs, arrived in the country on 2 August 1948 and were given Turkish Serials 7251 to 7350. These were later supplemented by eighteen ex-RAF Harvard Mark IIBs from the Royal Norwegian Air Force, six arriving on 4 October 1955 and twelve more on 6 November 1955. They received the Turkish Serials 7351 to 7368. These were followed, on 18 July 1956, by a further eight Mark II Harvards that arrived from RCAF sources and were numbered 7369 to 7376.

Under the NATO Mutual Air Programme Turkey received yet further batches of North American COIN and trainer aircraft. The first of these new assignments were sixteen former LT-6Gs. These arrived on 7 September 1957 and were assigned Serial Numbers 7277 to 7392. They were followed by three more of the same type on 7 October 1957 (7393 to 7395) along with eleven T-6Gs (7396 to 7399 and 7501 to 7505).

Two more consignments were shipped to Turkey in 1958. On 13 January of that year twenty-one machines arrived and were numbered 7508 to 7528), while on 5 May 1958 a final batch of nineteen were received (7529 to 7547).

All these aircraft served on the Turkish Air Force Inventory for over twenty-five years, the final T-6 being phased out in 1976. (*Author's collection, courtesy of Turkish Air Force, Ankara*)

The use of Harvards/T-6s for Military COIN (Counter-Insurgency) and close-support aircraft was widespread post-war. One of the foremost users of such machines in this role was the Portuguese Air Force. Many were used thus in the Angola conflict, a few falling victim to the shoulder-launched Soviet SAM-7 missiles supplied to the Communist guerrilla forces.

The final combat usage of the Harvard however, was closer to home, when, on 11 March 1975, two of them (1737 being one of these) were used to bomb an Army barracks close to Lisbon during an abortive coup against the new Government which had overthrown the old right-wing ruling party the year before. Three years later the type was finally withdrawn from official combat usage and many were sold overseas.

Fortunately, thanks to the dedicated work of Colonel Fernandes Nico, commandant of *Base Aerea 6* at Montijo, who recovered and maintained T-6J 1774, the *Museu do Ar* at Alverca was persuaded to save two of these machines in airworthy condition. The FAP staff at another airfield, *Base Aerea 7* at San Jacinto, hid a second machine (1769) away from the scrappers and ground-ran the engine at frequent intervals to keep it serviceable.

Eventually Colonel Nico was allowed to add this to the first machine together with a large stock of T-6 spares. Both are airworthy and hopefully can be kept flying for another decade yet. Here 1769 is seen over the Portuguese coast in 1989, the underwing machine-gun pods and rocket launchers can be clearly seen under the nearside wing in this photograph. (*Courtesy J. Laneiro, Lisbon*)

Right up to the present day the T-6 has proved itself a popular choice for the entertainment industry also. From early wartime black and white motion picture epics, like *I Want Wings*, which starred Brian Donlevy and Veronica Lake, through to wide-screen film presentations like *Tora, Tora, Tora* and *The Battle of Midway*, and on through the TV series *Black Sheep Squadron* (as suitably willing victims of 'Pappy' Boyington's Marine Corps Chance-Vought Corsairs), the T-6 has been filmed.

At first in its original authentic form, but more recently, they were modified with new cowling, rudders, canopies, wing-tips and paint-jobs to double-up, almost endlessly, as Japanese Mitsubishi Zero fighters, Nakajima Kate torpedo-bombers and a whole host more, at Hollywood's behest. They have become mock Republican Thunderbolts in *A Bridge Too Far*, (featuring similar checkerboard cowling markings to N2861G which is shown here, in a photograph taken at Van Nuys airfield, California in July 1968, although without the tail gun!) and metamorph-ised into Soviet Yaks. T-6s have been altered and disected for all manner of aerial imitation and promotion. (*Courtesy Nick Williams Collection*)

The *Marine Luchtvaartdienst* (Royal Netherlands Navy) obtained six Harvard Mark IIBs from the Royal Netherlands Air Force on loan in 1946. After three years they were returned. A further four were similarly loaned from 1958 onward and a final quartet were transferred at de Kooy in 1965 and 1966. Although the lion's share of the Dutch Harvards job was, of course, advanced training for air force pilots, a small number were used for communications and courier services, *Basisvlucht* duties. Six camouflaged Harvards, stationed at Deelan airbase, formed a photographic flight and had a reconnaissance task. In addition to military training further Harvards were also used as a training aircraft for civil pilots.

Here maintenance work is taking place on one such Harvard. The overall paint scheme has now reverted to the traditional NATO yellow with black markings. (*Author's collection, courtesy Royal Netherlands Air Force*)

An underside look at a trio of French Harvards. The French air force had first received replacement for all the T-6s lost in 1940, when three ex-RAF Harvards joined a training establishment in Syria in 1943. In January 1944, a fighter transition school was established at Meknes, Morocco and its establishment included some T-6s. Towards the end of 1944 the RAF gave two more Harvards to the French air training school at Blida, Tunisia. These few relics remained the sum total strength in French service until the formation of NATO in 1949, then things changed dramatically.

A brand-new training base was established at Marrakech on 1 January 1949 ready for the T-6s. A second ATS flew Harvard IIs at Salon de Provence, southern France between 1949 and 1952. France received thirty Harvard Mark IIBs in April and May 1949 from the RAF. Under MAP the USAF was delivered a further 119 T-6Ds which joined training establishments in Morocco. In the same year, and under the same scheme, France also received fifty-one Harvard IIIs (forty-five via the USAF and six from the RCAF), also in Morocco. In 1952 the Aéronavale, also under MAP and also in Morocco took delivery of fifty-six SNJs and a further seventeen Mk IIs arrived from Canada. A fresh batch of forty-nine AT-6Ds arrived here between October 1951 and April 1952, some of which survived until 1958 when the unit moved to Tours. Odd machines also served at the Rochefort and Saintes Mechanics' schools as static airframe workshops in the 1950s and flew from the Cazaux Test Centre on liaison duties in the same decade.

With Moroccan independence the French school was moved to Cognac in September 1961 and the Texans continued to train 200 French pilots a year until phased out of service in 1965 when they were replaced by Fouga Magister 170 jet trainers. (*Courtesy SIRPA/ECP Armées, Fort D'Ivry, Paris*)

Final notes on the Dutch use of the North American trainer was when a further forty ex-RCAF Harvards were delivered to the Netherlands East Indies in August 1948, two of which were damaged in transit. They were flown as trainers at the flying schools at Kalidjati. Those that survived were handed over to the Indonesian Republic in 1950 on independence.

Here an echeloned stack of Royal Netherlands Air Force Harvards is caught over the south of the country in immaculate formation. (*Author's collection, courtesy Royal Netherlands Air Force*)

The *Fliegerabwehrtruppen* (Swiss Air Force) purchased forty Noorduyn-built Harvard IIBs from the RCAF in 1947 and these were given the Swiss Serials U-301 to U-340. On their arrival in Europe they were given a complete overhaul by the Dutch firms of Aviolanda and Fokker of Amsterdam and Schipol. From 1949 to 1968 they served with great success as blind-flying instruction machines, for, in this period, practically all military trainee pilots obtained the blind-flying qualification. They were employed strictly as training and liaison aircraft and no armament was *ever* carried. (*Author's collection, courtesy of Swiss Air Force*)

The ultimate stretching and modification of the T-6 having already been achieved, North American continued to widen its range of alternatives building on its acknowledged solid base for training aircraft. The ultimate wartime result of all their experience was this machine, the X-SN2J-1 experimental Scout/Trainer aircraft developed by North American in 1945 for the US Navy.

It featured a whole host of innovations which wartime training programmes had shown to be desirable. The adoption of the double-bubble canopy improved all-round vision for both pupil and instructor, while a whole range of automatic devices were built-in to the rear cockpit to enable the teacher to simulate all manner of 'emergencies' to be practised for in advanced training modes. As at this stage of the war the desirability of combining functions to effect cost savings was obviously desirable, the defeat of the enemy being clearly only a matter of time and the wartime budgets would obviously be severely cut-back, the same observation qualities were directly applicable to aircraft with a scouting role. However, this type had already been combined with the dive-bomber in the US Navy and there was no longer a requirement for a separate type. (*Courtesy of Rockwell International Archives*)

100

6 Re-Birth and Re-Generation

In the United States the advance training programme had followed broadly similar lines to those conducted by the British in Canada and Rhodesia and the Australians at home except it was on a larger scale and more lavish. The qualified pilot requirement rose from 30,000 in October 1941 to 50,000 a year later. American Cadets went through four stages, Primary, Basic, Advanced and Transitional. The AT-6 Texans performed the Advanced role at the beginning of the 1940s with the Stearman PT-17 (a biplane and the American equivalent to the British Tiger Moth), along with the Fairchild PT-19 and Ryan PT-22 (both monoplanes) performing the Primary roles, and the Vultee BT-13A carrying out the Basic training function. The British Commonwealth Air Training Plan training system left out the Basic stage completely and moved the '65-hour Student' straight on to the Harvard from Tiger Moths or Fleet Finch Primary trainers. The Americans later adopted this approach. From 1943 onwards the influx of powerful modern fighter aircraft like the Chance Vought Corsair and Republic Thunderbolt hitched requirements and expectations up a notch and the students moved straight on to the AT-6, which took over the Basic training role for a more realistic scenario.

British and Canadian pupils were trained in the Harvard, but the only real difference in the machines were that the modern American style pistol-grip control moulded to the hand and fingers, was replaced by the old-style RAF style circular stick-grip, which again reflected the different fighter controls of the respective nations. The Harvard also had a circular compass of imposing size and weight let into the cockpit floor instead of the neater console-mounted AT-6 version. By 1943-44 the influx of hopeful pilots far exceeded the requirement or needs of the Allies, who had an abundance of trained and skilled pilots to spare, but were desperately short of foot soldiers on the ground. Subsequently there were wholesale cutbacks in entries in both nations and many cadets had their flying careers abruptly terminated before they ever began. This policy was naturally paralleled in the requirement and needs of the training aircraft themselves, and many AT-6/SNJ/Harvard orders were cancelled. Many others in the USAAF, RAF, RCAF and others air arms were assigned to combat squadrons as 'Hacks' and spent their whole lives a personal taxi and stores shifters for senior personnel. Canadian-built Harvards and Australian-built Wirraways alike saw service in the USAAF and a hopeless mix of types, marks and serials resulted. At the time it seemed unimportant, only in retrospect does the tracking down of individual aircraft histories seem essential to the enthusiast.

The ending of World War II saw the disposal of hundreds of AT-6s, Harvards and the like at knock-down prices. As in most such cases disarmament was rapidly carried out by war-weary governments, too hastily carried out as events were to prove only too quickly. There were bargains aplenty with such a short-sighted policy, often perfectly airworthy aircraft being sold for under five hundred dollars. Both foreign governments and civilian aviators benefitted from this, but within a few years the realities of the Cold War saw a reversal of thought and the T-6 (as it was re-designated by the USAF in 1947) was to undergo a startling change of fortune.

The disposal programmes and immediate post-war career of the Texans is similar for most of the larger nations therefore. Let us examine them alphabetically merely for convenience sake.

Very few Wirraways survived for preservation, those that have are featured in these pages. The fate of the Boomerang was to be similar. Production ceased with A46-105 in June 1943. Boomerangs had served with No.2 OTU at Port Pirie, SA and Mildura, Victoria from 10 October 1942 onwards, but their careers were relatively brief. No. 84 Squadron had ceased to use the Boomerang as early as 15 October 1943, No. 8 Communications Unit flew its last Boomerang sortie on 5 August 1944 and next to give up the machine was No. 85 Squadron until 27 January 1945. The remaining operational units were not far behind, with Nos 4, 5 and No. 83 Squadrons all ceasing to fly Boomerangs from 15 August 1945.

One Boomerang survived, the Mark I A46-30. This aircraft was the thirtieth production aircraft built and was completed in February 1943. It had its initial forty-five-minute flight from Fisherman's Bend on 2 February and then was flown to No 1 Aircraft Depot at Laverton where it was handed over to the RAAF three days later. After the usual checks the Boomerang was sent to No 2 OTU at Mildura and then to No. 83 Squadron at Strathpine, Queensland on 20 April. During the mythical 'Japanese Task Force' scare A46-30 was one of the many aircraft hastily flown to reinforce No. 85 Squadron at Guildforth, Perth, on 6 May.

Routine patrol, convoy escort and fighter training missions followed and after a rough landing had resulted in a wing replacement the aircraft underwent repairs and maintenance before rejoining No 85 Squadron on Christmas Eve 1943. Another accident occurred on 5 July 1944 involving replacement of the port wing. Further brief service with No. 85 Squadron was followed by storage at No 4 Aircraft Depot, Kalgoolie, WA from 11 December 1944 until 21 March 1945. A46-30 then joined No. 83 Squadron at Menagle, Sydney, NSW for home defence duties.

An interesting interlude followed when it was disguised as a Lockheed Altair aircraft for a film about Charles Kingsford-Smith which was being shot. Its regular pilot Warrant Officer Brian Thompson flew it for several sequences. Thus it survived when all of No 83 squadron's other Boomerangs went to the scrapyards at Tocumwal on 24 September 1945. A46-30 on the other hand went to Richmond for ten months before being handed over by the Australian Government to the Australian Air League at the Cabramatta Company's base near Sydney on 29 August 1946.

For the next two decades it rotted away at Blacktown NSW and was vandalised. Not until 1964 did Richard Hourigan persuade Wing Commander Keith Isaacs at Williamstown to obtain the aircraft back from the Air League to save it from a final demise. This was done and restoration was commenced at Williamstown where it was placed on display two years later. In April 1977, forty-three years after it had left Fisherman's Bend A46-30 returned there and CAC under project officer Ian Royle, who faithfully restored it and it also is a static display at the Australian War Memorial.

The crop-spraying derivative, the Ceres, met similar indifference, although just as unique an aircraft. The full list of Ceres aircraft and their original owners is given here for historical records as follows:

CA28-1*	VH-CEA (VH-CEX)	Proctor's Rural Services
-2	-CEB	Airfarm Associates
-3	-CEC	Airfarm Associates
-4	-CED (ZK-BPU)	Aerial Farming, NZ
-5	-CEF (VH-SSZ)	Coondair Tintinara SA
-6	-CEG	Airfarm Associates
-7	-CEH (ZK-BXW)	Aerial Farming NZ
-8**	-CEI (ZK-BXY)	Aerial Farming NZ
-9	-CEL (ZK-BZO)	Cooksons Airspread NZ
-10	-CEK (VH-SSY)	Airfarm Associates
-11	-CEM (ZK-BVS)	Wanganui Aerowork
-12	-CEN (ZK-BVS)	Aerial Farming NZ
-13	-CEO (VH-SSF)	Marshall Spreading Service
-14	-CEP (VH-DAT)	Doggett Aviation WA
-15	-CEQ (VH-WAX)	Airland Improvements

-16	-CER	Marshall Spreading Service
-17	-CET (VH-WHY)	Airland Improvements
-18	-CEX (VH-SSV)	Airfarm Associates
-19	-CEU (VH-WOT)	Airland Improvements
-20	-CEV	New England Aerial Top Dressing
-21	-CEW	Airfarm Associates

* This aircraft rebuilt and became CA28-18
** This aircraft was written off in a crash.

Back in the military field with the T-6G, the revitalisation of the Texan through the NATO policy of the late 1940s brought a new generation of pilots into contact with this aircraft.

Although not directly a part of this revitalised NATO policy North American themselves took advantage of the situation to upgrade the Texan themselves. They saw the need for a cheap and reliable aircraft, moderately armed for ground support and anti-guerrilla warfare operations which could be a cheap form of air support for poorer nations in the troubled post-war world of nationalistic and communist-inspired rebellion.

Accordingly, a solitary FT-6G was built as a Counter-Insurgency (COIN) prototype to test the market. Underwing pods carrying .30 calibre machine-guns were fitted, along with ground-strafing potential with racks for up to 400lb of bombs, rockets and napalm containers being fitted. This idea never took-off, but the concept was basically a sound one and similar adaptations were later made by a variety of air forces around the world, as we shall examine later.

The T-28-C showing the three-bladed propeller, the tricycle under-carriage, bubble canopy and marked dihedral of the wings, strengthened and extended tail fairing which showed the way for the final generation of post-war prop trainers and the final transition between prop and jet training requirements of the late 1940s and early 1950s. Although a very different machine to the old T-6 the ancestry can clearly still be traced. (*Courtesy of Rockwell International Archives*)

The reconstructed Royal Netherlands Air Force received 150 Harvard Mark IIBs from former RAF stocks plus fifty more from the RCAF between August 1946 and November 1948. In this photo a batch of these can be seen undergoing stringent overhauls at the factory of Aviolanda/Fokker before entering Dutch service. In addition another twenty former RAF Harvards were purchased from training school surplus stock in South Africa and shipped via the UK in February 1947 for use as spares. They were used as advanced trainers and later some were utilised for communications aircraft. The final Harvards were withdrawn from service in 1968. (*Courtesy Arthur Pearcy Archives*)

A beautiful in-flight view of a United States Air Force T-6G (TA-143 – 93143).

The wholesale post-war disposal and scrapping programme embarked upon with such enthusiasm in 1945 came to a halt with the establishment of NATO in the face of the Soviet take-over of Eastern Europe and its massive threat to the rest of that continent. A crash programme was therefore started to refurbish and modernise 2,068 of the T-6Cs and T-6Ds that remained on the new United States Air Force's inventory.

This programme resulted in the T-6G variant. The type was given a North American NA designation as the NA-168, although, in reality these were not new production models at all. For the Air Force all the airframes finally taken in hand for modernisation under this scheme, were re-built by the parent company. Full-scale modernidation took place at four plants, each factory having its own identifying code letter added to the serials, North American's Downey (NI) and Fresno (NF), the Douglas plant at Long Beach (NA), all in California, and the former Curtiss plant at Columbus, Ohio (NH), although for a short time these were designated as T-6Hs.

The outward and visible changes were relatively slight. Mid-bracing was removed from the cockpit canopies and replaced by larger clear-panels for much improved visibility. All provision for machine-gun armament was removed. The 550 hp Pratt & Whitney engine still remained as the -G's power plant and the modest streamlining did not push up the speed above 205 mph. (*Courtesy of Rockwell International Archives*)

Under the same programme the US funded the successor of Noorduyn, the Canadian Car and Foundry Company, to refurbish some 285 Harvard Mk.IVs to a similar standard under the Mutual Defense Assistance Program (MDAP). Once completed most, although not all, of these T-6Js, were assigned to help rebuild the NATO air forces of Belgium, France, Italy and West Germany. From 1951 onward also, the Canadians also engaged on a fresh construction programme on their own account, utilizing available material, engines and parts on hand. Some forty of these machines, designated as the Harvard IV, were completed at the Fort William, Quebec, plant of CCF. The modifications followed almost exactly the -G programme across the border. They were followed by a further 515 of the same specification, built from scratch. Again, under MDAP American funds purchased no less than 285 of these and supplied them to European air forces as the T-6J.

This beautiful air-to-air photograph of Royal Canadian Air Force trainers from Goderich was taken in 1955 over Lake Huron. Note the leader's bands on the nearest aircraft's tailfin and rudder. (*Canadian Forces Photographic Unit, Ottawa*)

Between 1948 and 1953 the Royal Australian Navy (RAN) also acquired and used sixteen Wirraways (for which the designation CA-20 is said to have originated) for both pilot and ground crew training at HMS *Albatross*, the Naval shore base located at Nowara, New South Wales. Of these A20-28 served with No. 723 Squadron; A20-133 and -139 with Nos. 723 and 816 Squadrons; A20-141 with No. 805 Squadron, A20-145 with No 723 Squadron and was written-off after an accident on 18 June 1953, A20-168 with Nos. 723 and 724 Squadrons, A20-176 with No. 723 Squadron, A20-209, -211, -214, -225, -237, -250 and -469 with Nos. 723 and 724 Squadrons, and A20-490 and -752 with Nos. 723 and 724 Squadrons.

None of the RAN Wirraways were ever utilised for deck landing training, although tail codes were allocated, NW for Nowara, K the aircraft-carrier HMAS *Sydney* and Y, then M, the aircraft-carrier HMAS *Melbourne*. All the RAN Fleet Air Arm Wirraways were finally sold off at disposal to Lund Aviation Inc., of New York, USA during 1957. None has ever re-appeared on the US Civil Register so it is assumed that these aircraft were purchased merely for the engine and propellers and were scrapped *in situ*.

This is A20-168 (972) of the Royal Australian Navy parked outside 'J' hangar (near the stop butts) at RAN Air Station Nowara in 1950. (*Official Royal Australian Navy Photograph*)

A final commercial spin-off from the Wirraway led to a continuation of the type in civilian hands despite the Government restrictions. This was the CA-28 Ceres Agricultural aircraft. It should be emphasised right from the start that the Ceres was *in no way* a modified Wirraway. Some Wirraway components fully inspected and in perfect condition were modified and incorporated into the Ceres but in all other respects it was a new design, built specially for agricultural work. Nonetheless the linage with North American's original product is there, however distant and tenuous.

Two prototypes were built and tested before production was commenced. The performance of the prototype Ceres A gave a maximum speed of 140 knots, a cruise speed of ninety knots and a landing speed of forty-seven knots. There was little change in performance of the production Ceres although the gross weight was increased to 7,410 lb. The standard Ceres Model B was fitted with the Wasp-geared engine and a DH Hamilton propeller, while Model C had the same engine type but with a 'high solidity' propeller. On aircraft number six and subsequent aircraft, the cockpit enclosure was extended aft to enclose a rear passenger compartment. The extended enclosure had clear acrylic panels each side and faired at the aft end with a hinged aluminium alloy door which swung sideways for access. The Ceres gained DCA approval for pilot and two passengers.

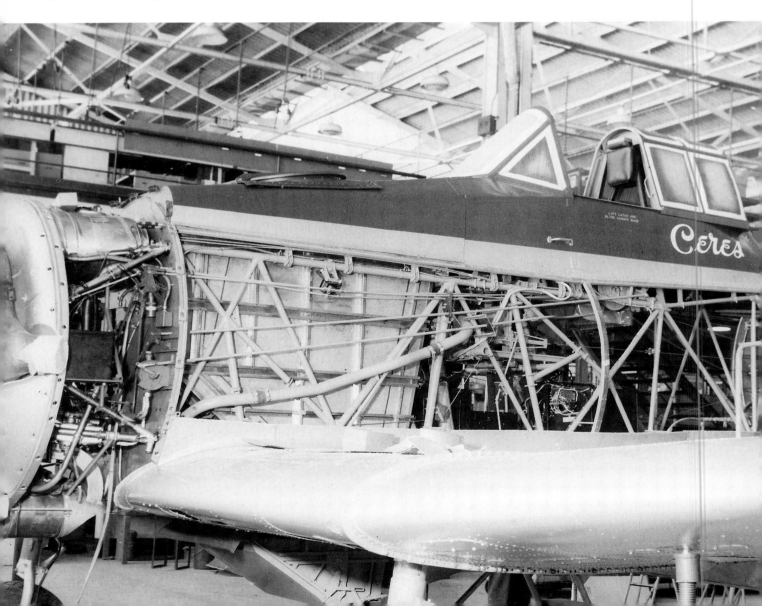

For the new post-war generation of US Navy pilots training continued from Pensascola, with the big carrier *Wasp II* (CV.18) acting as training deck for a period and giving a broader expanse of deck for the cadets to practise alighting upon than the old *Charger*, with her stubby, confined flight-deck, had offered their fathers. Even the big brand-new 'Midway' class carriers were hosts to SNJs from time-to-time, and their decks were broad enough for aircraft to land side-by-side.

The date is 14 September 1953 and a double-landing involving an F4U and a SNJ takes place aboard the United States Navy aircraft-carrier *Franklin D Roosevelt* (CVA 42). The SNJ (878) has taken the arrester wire succesfully on the right-hand side of the flight deck as the Chance Vought Corsair (308) with arrester hook extended, thumps down on the teak a few seconds later to the left.

The final flight of the SNJ-7 took place from Barrin Field, Alabama, on 14 March 1958. Apart from Air National Guard units, one official user in the States continued to fly Texans for a few more years yet and that was 35 Air Rescue Squadron, part of the US Civil Air Patrol. This unit was Uncle Sam's last contact with North American's finest product. (*US Navy photo, Courtesy National Archives, Washington, DC*)

(left)

The wholesale disposal and scrapping programme embarked upon with such enthusiasm in 1945 came to a halt with the establishment of NATO in the face of the Soviet take-over of Eastern Europe and its massive threat to the rest of that continent. All of a sudden it was not a safe world after all and one demise of one awful dictator had resulted merely in his being supplanted by an even more dreadful one. Early in 1950 stock was taken of the run-down arsenals of the west and among the many deficits were adequate training aircraft to fuel the new aerial expansion of the USA and her NATO allies. A crash programme was therefore started to refurbish and modernise 2,068 of the T-6C and T-6Ds that remained on the new United States Air Force's inventory, along with fifty Navy SNJs, to fill the gap until new types could take the strain. (Incidentally, due to shortages of available stock, it also meant in some cases the re-purchase of recently disposed-of airframes at vastly inflated prices, such has always been the military way!)

The outward and visible changes brought about by the refurbished American T-6Hs were relatively slight. Mid-bracing was removed from the cockpit canopies and replaced by larger clear-panels for much improved visibility. All provision for machine-gun armament was removed. The 550 hp Pratt & Whitney engine still remained as the -G's powerplant and the modest streamlining did not push up the speed above 205 mph.

In Canada the story was somewhat different. The Canadian Car and Foundry company built no less than 555 Harvard IVs brand-new from 1951 onwards. Apart from the elongated exhausts on the right-hand side and cockpit canopy strutting and appearance, the only difference between them and the American T-6H modifications was the much less prominent ADF antenna abaft the instructor.

Here an immaculate formation of the new Harvard IVs belonging to the Royal Canadian Air Force are seen on one of the last 'official' training flights by these machines. (*Canadian Forces Photographic Unit, Ottawa*)

(above)

A CA-28 Ceres Agricultural aircraft comes in to land. The Australian farmers and graziers were among the earliest to promote crop spraying from the air. In terms of ease of use and cost they were soon convinced this was the way to go. It must be remembered that the adverse environmental aspects were not to the forefront of people's thoughts in the late 1940s and 1950s as they are today. By 1959, well over two million acres were being treated with super-phosphate, seed, insecticides, herbicides and other materials from the air.

With such a startling growth in the industry the need for an Australian designed aircraft became obvious. The CAC investigated all aspects of this problem placing the emphasis on first cost, safety and economical operation. The result was the Ceres concept. By good design and the utilization of some components of the Wirraway Trainer, the Ceres could be produced for a selling price of 14,000 Australian pounds.

The wing area was 312 square feet, the fixed slats on the outer half of the wings and large slotted flaps resulted in excellent flying characteristics right down to the stall (at fifty knots) which was entirely without vice. The wing loading in the normally fully loaded condition of 6,900 lb was 22.1 lb per square foot. The Pratt & Whitney engine was fitted with a three-bladed Hamilton propeller. The Ceres was sold in both Australia and New Zealand, and twenty-one machines were registered. (Only twenty were actually built, the extra machine being a re-build after a crash.)

Span was 46ft 11 inches, overall length 30 feet 8½ inches, height 12 feet 5 inches and ground angle 12 degrees 54 minutes. It had a wheel track of 12 feet 6¾ inches and fuel capacity of eighty Imperial gallons. The Ceres had a two hour endurance and a landing ground run of 175 yards. Cruising speed was 110 knots, with a rate of climb of 1,520 feet per minute and a range of 500 nautical miles.

Although only a handful of the Ceres type were built before production ceased, their usage was to have useful repercussions. (*Courtesy Hawker de Havilland, Melbourne*)

And so into the 1990s and the T-6 had undergone yet a third re-birth, this time as one of the most popular flying veteran aircraft of all time with civilian owners and Warbird Associations. This renewed popularity should see the Texan, in all its many guises, gracing our skies (and deadening our eardrums) well into the 21st Century, a fact that 'Dutch' Kindelberger and his small team could hardly have predicted back in 1937!

We have seen how tight were the restrictions placed on the former military Wirraways in Australia and how limited was their subsequent civilian role post-war as a result. By way of strict contrast, in the United States one of the most common outlets for former AT-6 and SNJs was the commercial, rather than the sport and pleasure, fields. That is not to say that the latter did not predominate, but they tended to be individualistic efforts.

Apart from National Guard duties (which by 1947 had become the Air National Guard or ANG), the popularity of the T-6 in the civilian field extends back to the immediate post-war era. Although the commercial aspect of its use has naturally declined with increasing running costs (with the Pratt & Whitney guzzling up half a gallon of fuel each minute) and shortage of spares, the private use for pleasure and sport has grown steadily ever since.

An excellent aerial study of N5500V, an SNJ belonging to the famous Confederate Air Force collection. (*National Archives, Washington DC, courtesy of Dr Ira Chart*)

The CAC Ceres was an all-metal, low-wing monoplane powered by a 600 hp Pratt & Whitney Wasp R-1340 S3H1-G, nine-cylinder radial air-cooled engine. Agricultural loads of up to 2,327 lb of dust or 250 gallons of spray were carried in a stainless-steel hopper having a capacity of forty cubic feet and which was located over the centre of gravity, which gave negligible change in the aircraft's fore-and-aft trimming. An emergency dump gate jettisoned the entire load in a few seconds. The change to liquid load was made by replacing the dust gate with an assembly carrying the air-driven pump, valve and filter. This unit had a capacity of up to 120 gallons per minute. Discharge was through a spray boom forming the trailing edge of the flap, which gave an effective swathe width of ninety feet.

CAC gave careful consideration to the cockpit and pilot comfort in this little machine. Footsteps and handgrips on either side enabled easy entry and exit, and the all-round vision was particularly good. The flight controls were conventional for the period, trim controls for elevator and rudder were fitted. The flaps were operated by a cranked handle operating a screw jack, but the flaps could be left in an intermediate position during operations, being lowered for landing. In some Ceres aircraft extra seating accommodation was provided for a crew member in a ferry flight, behind the pilot and facing aft.

This particular Ceres (VH-SSF) was owned by Blaney Air-farmers of Bathurst, New South Wales and is pictured landing at the company air strip in March 1979. Note the increased wingspan, raised cockpit, fixed undercarriage and the hopper location. (*Copyright, 1979, N.M. Parnell*)

Although not completely docile, the Harvard lent itself to formation team work and was so exploited throughout its long career. The list of Harvard Display Teams in service use is a long one, and nowadays there are several formation teams which employ the good old 'Texan' or its derivatives to put on stunning spectacles all over the world at Meets and Fly-Ins.

This Canadian formation team shows their skills during a practice 'aerial dance' routine in the mid-1960s and shows what could be done with the Harvard in experienced hands. (*Courtesy Canadian Government Official Archives, Ottawa, Canada*)

The equipping of all the NATO air fleets post-war was conducted as part of the Allied policy of combined strength and included in this latter day post-war equivalent of 'Lend-Lease' initiated under the Marshall Plan were of course both refurbished T-6s and Canadian-built Harvard IVs.

A late model Texan, known as the T-6H, (MM54111 – AA-51) of the Italian *Aeronautica Militare* running up her engine at a training base in 1972. (*Author's collection via Official Italian Air Force Archives*)

Seen over the Rockies in 1961, these two Royal Canadian Air Force Harvards show very well the cockpit canopy differences between the Harvard IIIs and IVs although otherwise the machines have been re-furbished to the same standards.

Internally the changes on both these and their American T6-H cousins were more far-reaching and important. On the latter the fuel capacity was increased from 110 gallons to 140 gallons by the fitting of two 15-gallon bladder-type fuel tanks, one being located in each outer wing panel. The rear seat was raised by six inches. The communications equipment was up-graded with the fitting of multi-channel VHF and UHF equipment and an oval rugby-football shaped ADF receiver was fitted abaft the re-located aerial, now fitted behind the cockpit in the Harvard style and out of the pilot's line-of-sight at last. Even when slightly offset to the left this had been a retrograde fitting and it is to be wondered that it lasted as long as it did in the US-built Texans. After-all novice pilots had enough problems without such an unnecessary hindrance to vision. Landing the AT-6 over that great hump of a cowl was hard enough anyway and involved a kind of crab-wise progression down the runway until fully confident.

The power button system was also brought up to date with its replacement by direct actuation of both landing-gear and the wing flaps. Merely putting the gear handle to 'down' carried out the full landing-gear functions without any further intervention on behalf of the pilot. This meant the elimination of the hydraulic pressure gauge from the instrumentation layout. The later -F type tail-wheel locking/steerable system became standard on the -G. Under this system the tail-wheel was made free-swivelling by the pilot neutralizing the rudder pedals and pushing the control stick forward. This made for a much simpler operation and helped cut down on the Texan's passion for ground-looping. Final confirmation of their 'status' was the adoption of British Harvard-style all-over yellow paint scheme. (*Canadian Forces Photographic Unit, Ottawa*)

A CC & F-built Harvard IV shares the runway (and the limelight) with other veterans at Downsview airfield, Ontario, sometime in 1958.

There never was a Harvard IV in RAF service. The British Government had disarmed more completely, more quickly and more disastrously than had the Americans after 1945 and found themselves in the same mess a few years later. In fact they were in worse trouble, more directly threatened by Soviet expansion but with no cash in the coffers to rectify the situation as was done in Canada and the USA.

Great Britain had already liberally supplied Commonwealth and Allied air forces with batches of its own Harvards of various marks, both during and immediately after the war. The RNZAF took delivery of thirty-eight Mark Is, fifty-three Mark IIs, and forty-one Mark IIIs, while the South Africans were allocated 436 Mark IIs, and 197 Mark IIIs during the war. Immediately after the war fresh consignments were made of almost brand-new, straight from the stores, models to various friendly governments in Western Europe and also to help the newly-emerging independent air forces of the former empire as the latter disintegrated at an accelerating pace between 1947 and 1967. (*Canadian Forces Photographic Unit, Ottawa*)

117

In South Africa civilian Harvards have been rare until fairly recently, despite the preponderance of military machines still flying. There were some civil registrations many years ago but these civil markings were merely test registrations for Syrian Air Force examples, which were overhauled and refurbished by the Field company at Rand Airport.

In 1989 twelve former Mozambique Air Force Harvards (originally Frelimo, French and Luftwaffe aircraft) were at Syferfontein airfield awaiting sale 'as seen' on the civilian market. (*Courtesy L.S. Vosloo*)

Another South African Harvard, this machine (7569) belonged to the Central Flying School and was based at Dunnottar, some 1,000 miles from the Cape in the Transvaal. It is pictured here at Ysterplaat Air Force Base, Cape Town, in May 1989. It features an all-metal fuselage. and ailerons etc with yellow outer wings. This machine was repainted in 1987 in the World War II Joint Air Training Scheme colours and today is frequently seen, as a regular CFS aircraft, taking part in air displays around South Africa.

Already having the largest Harvard fleet in the world, the SAAF will probably be still flying them in 2000 AD.

The first civilian Harvards for many years were seen in South Africa in 1989, there were civil machines many years ago but these were merely civilian test registrations for some Syrian Air force examples being overhauled and renovated by the airwork firm of Fields at Rand Airport. Others were the twelve ex-Mozambique Air Force Harvard Mk IVMs (originally FAP and Luftwaffe machines) which ended up at Syferfontein airfield awaiting rebuilding for the civilian market.

Among the preserved machines is 7729, a Mark III Harvard, which was for a long while at Fort Klapperkop Military Museum, but which has more recently been transferred to the South African Airways Apprentice School. (*Courtesy L.J. Vosloo, Fish Hoek*)

To just what lengths a real enthusiast will go to build and fly their own T-6 is illustrated by the 1972 Grand Champion Warbird, an immaculate aluminium T-6 (N3682F), *How Sweet It Is* illustrated here on her maiden flight, which was built from scratch using new surplus parts from all over the USA by Dr Gerald A. Swayze of Mesquite, Texas. He later told the story of how it all came about.

'I looked at quite a few T-6s, but most left a lot to be desired. It was impossible to find one that didn't have zinc chromate peeling off on all the interior surfaces. Very few of them are clean and dent-free enough to look good with a polished aluminium exterior. Besides, I had always wanted a new T-6 and for that I had been born too late.

In 1968 at a C.A.F. Airshow, I saw a beautiful Bearcat, N-9G, the magnificent bird of Gunther Balz. This airplane gave me the inspiration I needed to begin the project that had been teasing my brain. Why not build a new T-6 with new surplus parts? So the decision was made and

N3628F with a run out engine was bought. In order to put together a new T-6, I would have to first tear an old one apart to see how to do it. Besides, some parts might be available and old ones, especially non-moving castings, could be made new.

Parts were secured from all over the country. The main suppliers were Don Wise and Southwest Aero Sales. A new left wing was unavailable so a used one was completely remanufactured at a cost of over 3,000 US dollars. I bought a new rear fuselage section, but decided to put a new skin on it because of numerous scratches from years of storage. I found five brand-new right wings in Dallas still in factory crates. Three of these wings were coated with cosoline and in mint condition. I still have two right-hand wings and don't know what to do with them.

(Courtesy Dr G.A. 'Doc' Swayze)

The South African Air Force has for a long time now retained the largest numbers of Harvards on its books of any air force in a variety of roles and seems likely to continue to operate this hardy veteran for some time yet! Parts and spares are not too difficult to come by and machines of various marks continue to be airborne on into the 1990s, a remarkable testimony to both the soundness of the original design and the versatility and resiliance of the type.

This photograph shows 7082 and 7406 on the ground at Swellendam airfields, in southern Cape Province, east of Cape Town, in September 1976. Both machines at that time belonged to No. 7 Squadron SAAF. (*Courtesy L.J. Vosloo, Fish Hoek*)

121

The burnished prop and yellow cowling of 'Doc' Swayze's first baby. He continues the story of how he assembled the necessary equipment after a nationwide hunt.

'A new wing center section was found and new gas tanks were installed. All of the parts in the center section are new including the landing-gear, wheels and brakes.

New engines were not to be found and I wanted a custom-built one anyway. How I ever got lucky enough to find Mr Faxel and Mr Cleveland of Fort Worth Engine Overhaul, I don't know. They did a magnificent job with the R-1340 An-1. It is the smoothest, most economical 1340 with respect to both fuel and oil consumption, that I have ever sat behind.

Initially, I thought it would take about three years to complete the project if I worked on it almost every day and that's hard to do when you are married and are a practising family doctor. It would have taken six years had I not had the constant help of Mr Redell Gross, who was also my pit man and crew chief from T-6 racing days.'

(*Courtesy Dr G.A. 'Doc' Swayze*)

The cockpit controls of 'How Sweet It Is'. If building the airframe and assembling the T-6 was difficult enough, getting it all wired up and passed fit to take to the air was a nightmare. Many would have given up at that stage, but 'Doc' stuck to it as he recalled later.

'The real monster in this project was the electrical system. I was determined to do it myself. To do so required that I learn soldering and the reading of electrical diagrams. It took four months and when later assembled all the goodies worked with the proper switch – that was a surprise. I really thought it would burn.

On May 14, 1972, I climbed into the cockpit for the test flight after Mr Bob Card made a thorough inspection of everything. I'll have to admit that after rigging the aileron boost tabs, it flies as pretty as it looks.'

Since then 'Doc' has gone from strength to strength and has re-built a further six AT-6s, three of which were remanufactured from primarily new surplus parts.

'I did not build these aircraft by myself, nor could have done so without the help of my loyal volunteer crew. They include Mr Redell Gross, Mr Tom Ryan, Mr Frank Goodloe, Mr Jim Walters and more recently Mr Dave Groark, who, by the way, flew 107 missions over North Vietnam. His SNJ-5 was the last aircraft we built, it is a sister ship to my latest one which is 5486V. It has the same paint scheme, which is Pre-World War II Navy from the Carrier *Saratoga*. Previously we had won 'Grand Champion Warbird Award' twice in 1972 and 1973.

(*Courtesy Dr G.A. 'Doc' Swayze*)

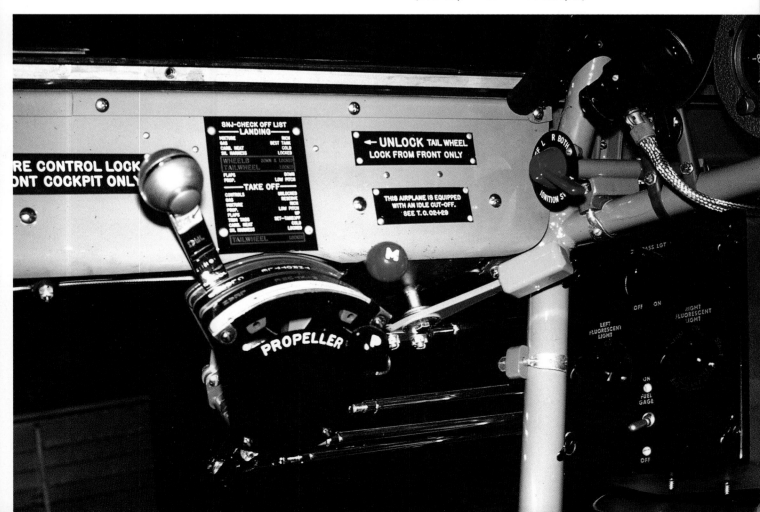

The home-built North American of 'Doc' Swayze shows her classic lines.
To get her in this pristine flying condition took a great deal of hard work,
improvisation and scheming as he relates.

'Much of the work was done at home. The garage was
scattered with parts. The study, upstairs, served as a
storage area for completed parts and sub-assemblies. The
cabinet in the den was full of completed small parts. Most
of the time there were T-6 parts on the bar in the breakfast
area.

My wife was then a school teacher of first and second
graders, and she was used to seeing toys peppered all over
and in general she was quite tolerant of it all. Once,
however, while doing the electrical system (wires were all
over the kitchen amidst dripping little balls of solder), I
saw her standing, hands on hips, tight-lipped with her right
foot tapping the floor. She got over it after I retreated with
my wires. I was finished anyway!'

(*Courtesy Dr G.A. 'Doc' Swayze*)

7 At War

And so the revitalised T-6G/SNJ-7 soldiered on into the 1950s and beyond in fresh guises as a training aircraft. The -Gs gave excellent value for money before they were finally phased out of the USAF and USN inventories. In the 1950s the Texans assumed the fresh duty for those who were part of the Training Command and became Primary Trainers (PTs). In this configuration rather than being the daunting third step on the road to being a pilot, as during the 1940s, the Texan was now thought docile enough to be the very first aircraft the novice took into the sky! After twenty hours (as against the WW II period of twelve to eighteen) of dual-control, aspiring aces went solo on the T-6. From there they graduated to the Lockheed T-33 jet trainer which began entering service in 1947. It was not until 1956 that the Air Force finally got rid of the sturdy Texan, which was 'officially' retired from duty at Bartow Air Force Base, Florida on 17 September of that year.

For the US Navy the story was much the same. The training continued from Pensacola, with the big carrier *Wasp II* (CV.18) acting as training deck for a period and offering a broader expanse of teak for the cadets to thump down on than the old *Charger*, with her stubby, confined flight-deck, had offered their fathers. The final flight of the SNJ-7 took place from Barrin Field, Alabama, on 14 March 1958. Apart from National Guard units one official user in the States continued to fly Texans for a few more years yet and that was 35 Air Rescue Squadron, part of the US Civil Air Patrol. This unit was Uncle Sam's last contact with North American's finest product. With the RAF also, in addition to such diverse duties as photo-reconnaissance, target-tugs, glider-tugs, instrument training, flying weather monitors, map-makers and the like, Harvards continued to be used as station hacks.

But before it finally departed from the USA and British military air scenes the incredible T-6 trainer was destined to carve further significant niches in combat history. In fact, the Texan and Harvards world-wide combat operations in the post-World War II period, if anything, *exceeded* their combat usage during that conflict. Also, following the lead set by the FT-6G, several nations produced their own versions of the Texan in a COIN role. Others made more primitive conversions to suit the immediate needs of the moment.

During the Korean War, when at first North Korea and then Communist Chinese Army divisions invaded South Korea and were resisted by United Nations' troops, the only modern aircraft that the victim nation had to defend itself with were two T-6Ds. The ROK Navy later modified a crashed T-6F by fitting the repaired wreck with floats from a former Japanese Nakajima A6M2-N ('Rufe') fighter seaplane and wingtip tanks from a F-80 Shooting Star jet. It entered service in 1951 as the one and only KN-1.

The ROK T-6s were utilised in strictly a training role and had no armaments. They continued to serve in this capacity and although the ROK Air Force was to be built up in the ensuring years it was in fact the USAF, USN and US Marine Corps, with help from the British Flect Air Arm Sea Fury fighter-bombers, who provided the bulk of the close-range air support for the troops on the ground with aircraft like the Mustang and Corsair. All the old lessons of such direct support, which had been so painfully learnt by trial-and-error during World War II, had to be virtually re-learnt from scratch and a fierce debate ensued over the accuracy and reliability of such air support. This was especially so when the new jet-powered F-80C Shooting Stars and F-84 fighter-bombers began to be extensively employed. Because of their speed, and also the lack of suitable training of the pilots, it was claimed by ground forces that they were at best inefficient, at worst downright dangerous to their own side.

The ground control and direction methods of World War II were re-introduced in the US 5th Air Force at this time but, following the example set by the Australian Wirraways in the last three years of the Pacific War, slower propeller-driven aircraft were employed as aerial Tactical Air Controllers or Target Spotters.

A special unit was set up, 6132 Tactical Air Control Group. General Earl Partridge is credited with adopting the old Australian ploy once more and it was put into effect on 10 July 1956 with three Stinson L-5G aircraft and seven officers based at Taejon air strip, which was described as, 'a loose gravel runway about the width of a country road and not much else'. It recognised early on, that the conventional observation and spotter/liaison aircraft, like the L-5 and the L-9, lacked both speed, ruggedness and efficiency in such a role. For this mission the reliable old Texan entered the conflict in new guise, as the LT-6G.

The first Texan to enter the fray was a re-built T-6C, a former hack of 35 Fighter Interceptor Group based in Japan. It had not flown for more than a year but was quickly given priority for refurbishment. The T-6 was kitted out with an AN/ARC-3 radio set capable of communication with both the ground controllers in the front line and the incoming fighter-bombers. This pioneer TAC reached Taejon on 10 July 1956 and was in action immediately, crewed by First Lieutenant James A. Bryant and First Lieutenant Frank Mitchell. Reserve was First Lieutenant Harold A. Morris. They quickly proved their value by locating a North Korean armoured column containing forty-two heavy tanks at Chochiown. Bryant signalled this news and the precise location to a formation of F-80Cs who arrived soon after to deliver a devastating rocket and strafing attack which knocked out seventeen of the enemy tanks. It was a stunning debut and the scouring of back-area bases for redundant T-6s began in earnest.

The T-6 pilots' duty was to patrol along the front-line and to report on enemy troop dispositions, movements and activity. A heavy responsibility lay with these flyers. The Air Force, Navy and Marine jets were only able to remain over the target for a matter of seconds due to the long ranges at which they operated and their short endurance. Moreover the heavy concentrations of light flak guns that the Communists assembled over vital objectives like bridges and artillery concentrations, made any lingering overhead a very risky and dangerous occupation. There was also the ever-present possibility of being 'jumped' by Yak-9 prop-driven fighters and later MiG-15 jets and it was not always possible to have a friendly North American Sabre on hand for protection. One 'Mosquito' pilot, Lieutenant Dick Meade, when he was 'jumped' by a Yak, fired his rockets at it in desperation, missing by yards but scaring the enemy fighter away.

Despite these hazards the lone Mosquito pilot had to accurately observe and mark the target for the fighter-bombers to strafe and bomb. They did this by precisely marking the enemy positions with 2½-inch smoke rockets and flares. These units gradually developed their skills and flew an enormous number of combat missions. On 15 July 5 Air Force HQ assigned a call sign to the FAC patrols that were stinging the enemy so badly, 'MOSQUITO'. The raucous noise of the T-6's Pratt & Whitney had only been slightly subdued by the fitting of a square-tipped propeller and was still a distinctive sound. The noise and the call-sign together made it inevitable that the FACs soon adopted the name by which they became famous, being dubbed the 'Mosquitoes'.

Although established and working, the 6132 had no 'official' status as a flying unit and found itself everybody's friend but nobody's baby. They received ample and heartfelt praise and congratulations but few supplies, little equipment, food, storage, fuel or support and had to scrounge aircraft and weapons as and how they could. They had grown to twenty-five personnel with twelve aircraft in varying states of readiness. Never has had the description 'ad hoc' formation been more suitably employed to describe a fighting unit operating in the fog of war!

The initial Communist onrush almost succeeded and the South Korean and UN forces were hemmed into the Pusan pocket, from where the 'Mosquitoes' operated as best they could from Taegu airstrip. Some three weeks after their first operational sortie the unit finally became a genuine USAF outfit when it was re-established as the 6147 Tactical Control Squadron (Airborne) on 29 July 1950. The commander of the new unit was Major Merrill H. Carlton. (He was to be relieved on 28 March 1951 by Colonel Timothy F. O'Keefe.) By the time they had become 'official' they had already flown 269 sorties in a three-week period.

For the next two months they continued to operate from Taegu. On some missions which required extremely close support the Mosquitoes used 1:50,000 maps to pinpoint targets within one hundred yards of friendly forces. In one such mission, against enemy troops holding the walled-city of Kasan, seven miles north of Taegu, and two adjacent ridges, a Mosquito directed a flight of B-26s over the target in a night mission in which the LT-6G pilot used his landing lights to expose the enemy target.

The position became fluid again for, with the breakout from Pusan by 5 Army, their bases became mobile once more. As the UN forces drove the North Koreans back behind their own borders and beyond in November, the Mosquitoes shifted base firstly to Seoul City airfield, South Korea, and then to Pyongyang East in North Korea, which they reached on 27 October in bitterly cold weather. In the period from 9 July to 25 November intensive operations were conducted and 4,902 combat missions were flown. By the end of August out of fifty-five pilots on the TAC(A) roster, seventeen had already completed a normal fifty mission tour of duty. The 6147 TCS(A) was credited with helping in the destruction of 436 enemy tanks, 598 artillery pieces and field guns, 2,332 soft-skinned motor transports, eight railway engines, twenty-seven ammunition dumps, ninety-eight fuel dumps and 228 supply dumps.

In one incident there had been a particularly heavy UN artillery barrage directed by the Mosquitoes onto a target near the Hwachon reservoir. The LT-6G overflew the target afterwards in the normal manner to assess results in preparation to directing the fighter-bombers onto any survivors. But by this time even the Chinese soldiers had got the message of what followed a Mosquito run! Enemy troops were observed clambering out of their trenches and foxholes and waving white sheets and clasping their hands on their heads in mute appeals of surrender. The Mosquito pilot quickly appraised the situation and, rather than waste good napalm on an already defeated enemy, directed the F-80 strike at fresh targets while the Chinese tramped over no-man's land to surrender in scores to the British troops opposite.

The intervention of massive Communist Chinese Army formations overwhelmed the extended UN forces by sheer weight of numbers and drove them back towards the 38th Parallel once more. The American President sacked General Douglas MacArthur when he requested Chinese targets be bombed to stem the flood and the retreat became a rout. The Mosquitoes once more had to pull back, again to Seoul and then south again to Chunchon airfield. Here they established themselves a main base for the first time in the war and were further expanded.

The Mosquito unit now became the 6147 Tactical Control Group which contained two Airborne squadrons, 6148 TCS (Western Sector) under Colonel Watson, and 6149 TCS (Eastern Sector) equipped with the modified T-6s, and one administrative, mechanical support and forward air control teams, as a general Ground squadron, 6150 TCS. The hastily-adapted AT-6Ds and AT-6Fs were gradually replaced with more sophisticated versions, especially modified for the work in hand. These were the LT-6Gs of which ninety-seven were eventually built. Their main difference over the basic T-6G was the additional radio communications equipment packed into the cockpit. They carried three basic sets, AN/ARC-3, AN/ARN-6 and SCR-522A. For target marking they were fitted with no less than six underwing racks capable of carrying three rocket launchers for either six 5-inch or eighteen 2½-inch white phosphorous smoke rockets each, while pods were slung under each wing fitted with two .30 calibre machine-guns for strafing opportunities. (These were later dropped to give a few knots extra speed over heavy flak concentrations.) Red identification stripes were marked diagonally across their wings for identification by friendly aircraft.

Against the now static front line, which settled down to a fair resemblance of the Western Front during World War I, the Mosquito units perfected their low-level reconnaissance patrol, identification and support techniques. Many pilots now commenced, and completed, a second tour of duty. The LT-6Gs sat in sandbagged revetments with engines running permanently on call. On one memorable day, 14 December 1950, no less than twenty-five machines were airborne on station at one time waiting for the fighter-bombers. The three-man ground teams (Tactical Air Control Parties) were equipped with jeeps and radio communications equipment. Each team comprised an officer, the Mosquito pilots rotated on this duty to gain experience, a radio man and a driver/mechanic. These teams spread out across the peninsular and kept in immediate contact with the Army's infantry and artillery HQs. They worked with the British, South Korean and other Allied troops as well as US land forces.

They were able to liaise directly with both ground troops and patrolling fighter-bombers and call in strikes independently themselves if the need arose. More often than not they called in the airborne Mosquitoes, one of which was kept over each half of the front line all the time, for aerial target identification and marking prior to the strikes, and aerial confirmation on the effectiveness of the attacks after the bombing and rocketing. The LT-6Gs duties also included artillery spotting, casualty evacuation, aerial photography, deep penetration, night direction of B-26s, directing naval bombardments, supply missions, long-range reconnaissance to study enemy build-ups behind the lines and limited interceptor roles against enemy observation aircraft, like the Soviet-supplied PO-2 night harassment biplanes. During lulls in operations some were fitted with DDT tanks and spray nozzles and used for fighting their namesakes which were a menace to local farmers and supplies during the summer months. Their work was honoured at the highest level on 4 February 1951 when the unit was presented with the Distinguished Unit Citation at Taegu West Airfield. A radio broadcast by the famous journalist Edward R. Murrow over the CBS network on 6 February, brought to the people back home news of what the LT-6Gs were doing in the almost forgotten war.

By the time the war petered out with the July 1953 cease-fire (it has never officially ended to this day) the Mosquitoes had lost forty-two of their aircraft to accident and ground fire, and thirty-three of their crew had been killed in action. The enemy concentrated their anti-aircraft fire power over the front, with the 20mm and 40mm pieces barraging at 3,000 feet and over while small-arms fire coned up to 1,200 feet. The Mosquitoes tried to operate in the narrow band in between those two parameters, but in reality there was nowhere to hide and it was rare for a mission to be completed without some ground-fire damage.

But the LT-6Gs conducted no less than 40,354 combat sorties and had helped with the destruction of enough tanks to equip five Communist armoured divisions as well as 563 guns and more than 5,000 soft-skinned untracked supply vehicles. It was an enviable record of dedication and service and one that crowned an already illustrious career.

The T-6 consistently broke aviation records in the States. With regard to its reliability, students at Craig Field, Alabama, a USAAF training unit, flew T-6s for 23 million miles without one single accident attributable to mechanical failure. At the other end of the scale another Craig Field T-6 showed what these aircraft had to endure in the course of routine training operations. This machine flew 2,000 hours during which time it was involved in eleven accidents, required seven new wings, five new landing-gear struts and six new propellers. During one intensive period the aircraft was in the air twenty-two hours a day. At Napier Field in the same state in October 1944, a Texan established the record for continuous service by completing 5,000 hours of flying time. This aircraft averaged three hours forty-five minutes flying time per day, or around 111½ hours per month and flew approximately 750,000 miles, (approximately thirty circumnavigations of the globe). Seven engine replacements were required in achieving this feat.

For adaptability the T-6 had few equals as we have seen. One duty it undertook was as a flying storm spotter with the US All-Weather Flying Center, known as 'The Hurricane Hunters'. A few Texans were reported fitted with skis for service in the Arctic and assisted in the rescue of crashed aircraft in Alaska, Greenland and Iceland. There was the instance of the floatplane version at Kwangji, Korea already mentioned. The machine successfully flew in August 1951 but was written off in a crash in November of the same year.

The SNJ trained some 40,000 Navy pilots during the war and the most decorated US Navy flyer of World War II, Lieutenant E. C. Dickinson, called the SNJ 'the best scout trainer in the world'. That sentiment was echoed and re-echoed by military pilots around the globe.

With the -G refurbishment programme begun on 5 October 1949, the USAF took 641 of the Downey remanufactured and modified T-6s (as the NA-168), and 59 LT-6Gs. The National Guard units took a further fifty. In the repeat order of 8 February 1951, 824 NA-182s were given the same treatment at Columbus. Long Beach-modified aircraft (NA-188s) were ordered on 11 April 1951 and totalled 107, and Fresno rebuilds (NA-195) from 19 March 1952 totalled eleven, with a further 110 T-6Ds brought up to -G standard (NA-197) for the National Guard at Fresno from 16 June 1952 onwards. The 240 SNJ-8s (NA-198) had their contracts terminated on 3 July 1952, as related, after some SNJ-6s had been updated to SNJ-7 by the US Navy Overhaul and Repair Facility at Naval Air Station Pensacola, Florida, in 1952.

In March 1956, 150 T-6GS were ordered by the French Air Force and they began to arrive at Bordeaux docks, ferried across the Atlantic on the decks of US aircraft carriers, in October of the same year. A second order of 150 was placed in November and others followed. Under the T-6G scheme no less than 693 of these re-manufactured trainers arrived in France.

Once landed, the French drastically modified these trainers to fit their new role. Armour plate was added to protect the crews from ground fire. The single nose-mounted .30 machine-gun was replaced by a heavier punch. There were two versions, one type equipped the T-6G with two 7.5mm guns, mounted in pairs on underwing pods, with four racks fitted under the wings for four SNEB 68mm rockets and six T-10 rockets and 110-lb bombs. The alternative payload comprised four 7.5mm machine-guns in underwing pods, two racks for 110lb bombs and four SNEB 68mm rockets and six T-10 rockets. Extra radio-equipment was fitted. Their aircrews underwent special ERALA conversion and training courses at Blida, Reghala and Caen. At their peak no less than thirty Texan-equipped ERALA squadrons were operational.

Once again that distinctive noise was heard in battle, this time over the desert wastes. And once more their unique howl brought about another nickname for the T-6 and they became known as 'Tomcats'. The Tomcats became the mainstay of close-support operations all through this bitter conflict up to 1961 and elsewhere. During that period they suffered the loss of 255 aircrew. They flew intensive missions and, by March 1957, had notched up 10,000 sorties. This total had increased to 106,512 during the first ten months of 1958, where they flew from seventy-two different airstrips and clocked up 115,000 flying hours.

With the end of the war the Tomcats' work was done and they were laid up for sale and scrap. Some went to private buyers and Air France bought a dozen for airline pilot training (sans weapons!). Others were returned to the USA. Many French Tomcats were sold to foreign air forces who had a need for such ground-attack aircraft, Morocco, Tunisia, Portugal, Spain and India. Unofficially, some found their way back into African war conditions in the hands of mercenary pilots during the Congolese and Biafran wars of 1964.

Sixteen Harvard Mk IIIs were transferred from the Royal Navy to the *Forca Aerea Portuguesa* (FAP – Portuguese Air Force) in March 1956. South Africa contributed fifty-nine more Mark IIA Harvards in 1969, while the Belgian Air Force transferred seven further Mark IIAs and three Mark IIBs. This batch was followed by another ten from the same source in 1962. Later additions include twenty surplus USAAF AT-6A and AT-6Bs, and twenty-five T-6Gs supplied under the Mutual Defense Assistance Program. In addition, the *Aviacao Naval* (Portugese Navy) acquired six SNJ-4s (Serials I-1 to I-6) from the USA and fifteen former Royal Navy Harvard IIIs which were handed over in 1956. Others (Serials 1701 to 1799) came in from sources as varying as Belgium, France and West Germany over the years. They were all used in their intended training role to start with.

Like most European powers with colonies Portugal had to fight several nationalist uprisings and wars in Africa and elsewhere post-war. They used armed T-6s in their colonial wars in Angola, where they proved very handy, but the introduction of Soviet-supplied SAM-7 shoulder-launched surface-to-air missiles soon showed up the vulnerability and several were lost. The COIN adaptations were also used in similar operations in Mozambique and Guinea up to August 1974.

The final (and most dramatic) combat action for the T-6 in Portuguese use was during the March 1975 uprising against the revolutionary government. Two machines bombed and strafed a loyalist Army barracks on 11 March, causing a large amount of damage. Those still employed as training machines were not finally withdrawn from combat operations until 1978.

Photographs showing Harvards actually dropping bombs are extremely rare indeed, hence the need to include this unique air-to-air shot in my collection for posterity. This is AJ596, a Mark II machine which initially served with 31 Service Flying Training School between May 1942 and May 1944, before being handed over to the Royal Canadian Air Force. She is pictured here in 1959. (*Courtesy R.C. Sturtivant*)

In actual war conditions the T-6 fought as hard with the French as with anyone. With the eruption of the Algerian uprising the *L'Armée de L'Air* began using converted AT-6Ds from the Marrakech school and then imported the huge numbers of T-6Gs to employ in the Ground-Support Light Aviation Command (ERALA) in the COIN role. The early conversions proved superior in this role to French types. They could operate from 800- metre long airstrips, had an endurance of almost five hours giving them a range of over 800 miles, and a relatively high cruising speed which, as the Mosquitoes had shown in Korea, were all commendable attributes, giving loiter time and ruggedness of operation in primitive conditions. (*SIRPA/ECPA France*)

During the war the Dutch pilots in exile were trained on RAF Harvards at Langham airfield in Norfolk. With the re-establishment of the *Koninklijke Luchtmacht* (Royal Netherlands Air Force) on its own liberated soil a flying training school was established at Gilze-Rijen airfield in 1946.

The Royal Netherlands Air Force took delivery of 200 Mark IIBs Harvard trainers from both the RAF and the RCAF in the immediate post-war years. This Dutch machine, (66) is shown with camouflage paint scheme overall, including the engine cowling as well as the standard national markings of the period. (*Author's collection, courtesy Royal Netherlands Air Force*)

Spanish T-6s disembarking from the US aircraft carrier *Corregidor* (CVE 58) at Santander in 1958.

Spain acquired her first batch of sixty AT-6D Texans when they arrived at Santander airfield between August and October 1954. They received the Spanish serials E.16-1 to E.16-60 and were basic aluminium coloured aircraft. They were destined for the training establishments at Matacan and Villanubla. The first unit to receive delivery was No. 74 *Agrupacion Aerea* while others modified for ground-attack work, went to the No. 3 *Cazabombardeo Tactico*.

During 1958 a second consignment of sixty aircraft was purchased, this time it was T-6Gs that were received. They were given the Spanish serials E.16-61 to E.16-120 and were used to replace the older models at both training centres and also those of the No. 3 Tactical Squadron.

During 1957 the situation in Spanish Morocco escalated and the *Ejercito del Aire* decided to utilised the older AT-6Ds as close-support aircraft to give assistance to the front-line F-86 Sabre jets. Between 1959 and 1963 these aircraft were refitted privately by the American firm Charlotte Aircraft Engineering to become almost brand-new machines. Seventy other machines were obtained, SNJ-4, -5 and -6 models, all of which were based at Matacan and other air bases. These new additions were given the Spanish serials E.16-21 to E.16-190.

In the COIN configuration modified AT-6Ds were equipped with wing-mounted Breda 7.7mm machine-guns and also had underwing racks capable of mounting a dozen Oerlikon ATG rockets or ten 221-lb bombs. This transformation was carried out at the AISA factory at Carabanchel and they were re-designated as C.6 Attack aircraft. (*Author's collection courtesy of Royal Spanish Air Force, Madrid*)

The T-6 saw considerable combat in the Korean War. The ground control and direction methods of World War II were re-introduced in the US 5th Air Force at this time but, following the example set by the Australian Wirraways in the last three years of the Pacific War, slower propeller-driven aircraft were employed as aerial Tactical Air Controllers or Target Spotters.

A special unit was set up; 6132 Tactical Air Control Group. General Earl Partridge is credited with adopting the old Australian ploy once more and it was put into effect on 10 July 1956 with three Stinson L-5G aircraft and seven officers based at Taejon airstrip, which was described as, 'a loose gravel runway about the width of a country road and not much else'. It recognised, early on, that the conventional observation and spotter/liaison aircraft, like the L-5 and the L-9, lacked both speed, ruggedness and efficiency in such a role. For this mission the reliable old Texan entered the conflict in new guise, as the LT-6G.

From their radio call-signs they became known as the MOSQUITO units. They proved brilliantly successful. As well as the target-marking Mosquito missions in Korea this versatile machine flew photo-reconnaissance missions over the front line. Here Major Angus J. Walker. DIR Photo Division of General Headquarters, Far East Command, poses ready to take-off on a T-6 Photo-recon mission near Taegh on 19 August 1950. (*US Army Photo, Courtesy National Archives, Washington DC*)

In the Korean War the Mosquito unit became the 6147 Tactical Control Group which contained two Airborne squadrons, 6148 TCS (Western Sector) under Colonel Watson, and 6149 TCS (Eastern Sector) equipped with the modified T-6s, and one administrative, mechanical support and forward air control teams, as a general Ground squadron, 6150 TCS. The hastily-adapted AT-6Ds and AT-6Fs were gradually replaced with more sophisticated versions, especially modified for the work in hand. These were the LT-6Gs of which ninety-seven were eventually built. Their main difference over the basic T-6G was the additional radio communications equipment packed into the cockpit. They carried three basic sets, AN/ARC-3, AN/ARN-6 and SCR-522A. For target marking they were fitted with no less than six underwing racks capable of carrying three rocket launchers for either six 5-inch or eighteen 2½-inch white phosphorous smoke rockets

each, while pods were slung under each wing fitted with two .30 calibre machine-guns for strafing opportunites. (There were later dropped to give a few knots extra speed over heavy flak concentrations). Red identification stripes were marked diagonally across their wings for identification by friendly aircraft.

LT-6Gs conducted no less than 40,354 combat sorties and had helped with the destruction of enough tanks to equip five Communist armoured divisions as well as 563 guns and more than 5,000 soft-skinned untracked supply vehicles. It was an enviable record of dedication and service and one that crowned an already illustrious career for the sturdy and surprising T-6.

North American T-6G, 42-86074A, K-16 at Seoul airport, South Korea on 23 May 1954. The unit markings are in yellow and black. (*Courtesy of Arthur Pearcy Archives*)

81573A.C. USAF Mosquito T-6 landing at a forward airstrip after making rocket strikes on Communist positions. (*Smithsonian Institute, Washington, DC*)

166862A.C. (AF3923.1) USAF armourer fitting smoke rockets beneath wing of Mosquito aircraft. (*Smithsonian Institute, Washington, DC*)

83699A.C. (SP2/30-272) Mosquito units at the revetments on a forward airstrip in Korea. (*Smithsonian Institute, Washington, DC*)

Two Tomcats patrolling the Sahara Desert. (*SIRPA/ECPA France*)

(*above*)
The cockpit layout of the preserved ex-Portuguese Air Force Harvard 1769 (ex 52-8565) at Montijo. This machine had in excess of 4,000 flying hours on the clock in 1989 and is still in flying condition after undergoing a detailed inspection in that year.

As well as the two fully airworthy examples preserved by the *Museu do Ar* 1769 (ex-52-8596) and 1774, there is another stored at Alverca in rather dilapidated condition, 1737. This machine is minus engine and the wings are dismantled, there is no propeller and the cockpit is incomplete. There are some hopes of restoration as a static display in the future. (*Courtesy J. Laneiro, Lisbon*)

(*below*)
A dozen or so former Mozambique Air Force Harvards used by the Frelimo, but also previously seeing service in the French and German air forces were located at Syferfontein after being declared surplus to requirements. They were all in a sorry state as these two photographs show.

They were all rescued in 1988 by a South African enthusiast, Brian Zeederberg, who purchased a job-lot and shipped them to South Africa. In 1989 three of these machines Nos. 1727, 1731 and 1751 were sold to South African Airways apprentice school, No. 1762 was sold in Durban, No. 1748 in Johannesburg and No. 1754 in Cape Town, all to civilian buyers, for approximately £15,000 each. (*Courtesy L.S. Vosloo*)

His instructor makes last-minute checks on his pupil before the take-off. A scene repeated a hundred thousand times in the T-6's long training career. Here the aircrew are Italian flyers of the *Aeronautica Militare* some time in the mid-1960s.

The first Italian Harvard was an ex-RCAG Mark II taken over from No. 15 MU, at Wroughton on 2 July 1947. The Italian air force subsequently received thirteen Harvard Mark IIs on 10 May 1949 (registered as T-6Ds on Italian records) via US allocation of acquired ex-RAF South African stock post-war. These joined the training school at Lecce.

Five further T-6s were delivered on 12 January 1951, four on 16 February, one of 14 March direct from the States. This gave a total of forty-three machines of which twenty-seven were operational. With the expansion of the Italian air force new schools were set up at Cagliari, Sardinia using Alhgero and Elmas airfields each with six aircraft. Further expansion took place in 1952 under NATO auspices and the first of a consignment of thirty T-6Gs began to arrive from America (some re-furbished AT-6Fs were included under the designation of T-6H). These were followed in 1953/54 by a further batch of sixty-nine Canadian Harvard IVs (also confusingly designated T-6H). A central flying school was also established at Foggia with eight T-6s, five of them operational. These machines continued to serve as basic trainers well into the 1960s.

The final 'official' Italian flight in a T-6 was made by Colonel Sergio Ponzio of 53 *Stormo* at 166.12 on 13 February 1979 from Cameri airfield. In actual fact a later (and highly unofficial) flight was made in an Italian Air Force Texan five days later by an anonymous Colonel from No. 330 *Gruppo*! (*Courtesy Aeronautica Militare, Roma*)

The T-6's commercial roles included civil airline pilot and general public aero training. The T-6 was widely used for crop-spraying in the States. A rather extreme example of re-building of two former SNJ-5s for this role which was carried-out by Bob Stroop. He ripped off the canopies and inserted a large chemical tank in the rear cockpit. Routine stuff, but to give the machine a slow, almost-hovering ability, he bolted a whole upper wing to struts on the lower wing and upper fuselage to produce two biplane variants, probably the only ones ever constructed anywhere. His customer was a crop-duster from Monroeville, Alabama, J.F. Carter who used them, precariously, for a number of years. They probably proved more successful than the specially-built CAC Ceres machines in Australia. These proved themselves rather expensive to run in practice and they needed a longer take-off and landing distance than usually available to crop dusters. In the event only twenty were ever built.

A more conventional SNJ-5 preservation is seen here sporting her 'Two-Star Admiral' markings over the modern aircraft carriers and guided-missile frigates of the US Fleet. (*Jim Larsen Photographs, Kirkland, Washington*)

142

8 At Work and at Play

Apart from the major nations' air forces, the T-6 has seen post-war service in a huge variety of roles in the inventories of military air arms all over the world since 1947. What is presented here is a brief summary of the most important of them.

On 18 March 1961, a squadron of eighteen Spanish C.6s was transferred *en mass* from Villanubia to Jerez to form No. 7 *Buchones del Ala*. These machines were used against guerrillas in Spanish Sahara desert colonies during the 1970s. The final ten Spanish Texan acquisitions came from the French *l'Armée de l'Air* surplus stocks of T-6Gs, which arrived in 1965 and received the Spanish Serials E.16-191 to E.16-201.

In 1974 the AT-6Ds were pulled out of the Sahara colony being replaced by Mirage F-1Cs for close-support. The -Ds continued to be used for reconnaissance and observation duties. By 1976 the greater part of the remaining -Ds were assigned to No. 90 *Escuadrillas Grupo* at Getafe and as various air base hacks. During their final service days at San Javier the survivors were re-designated as the CE.6.

The T-6Gs that remained as training aircraft were used by 741 and 742 *Escuadrones* at Matacan until 1972 when the unit was transferred to San Javier and formed the 793 *Escuadron*. They were ultimately replaced in the training role by the CASA C-101 type.

Subsequently the Air Force Aerobatic team performed with these T-6s for a considerable period. The last official flight by Spanish Air Force T-6s took place from 31 June 1982.

The Belgian Air Force took delivery of fifty-six Mark IIA and Mark III Harvards between February and May 1947 which came to them from South Africa via the UK. Most of these aircraft were flown from UK to Brustem airport which had hardly re-emerged from its wartime devastation. Ten Mark IIB Harvards were received in August to October 1949, along with one from the Royal Netherlands Air Force, with another ten arriving from Britain between September and October of the following year. Between October 1952 and March 1953 ten more were received from the Dutch.

Two dozen more Mark IIA Harvards were added to the Belgian fleet in November 1953, being surplus to British requirements with the closure of the RATG. An advanced flying school was set up at Kamina in the Belgian Congo to take advantage of all-round climate conditions in a similar manner to the British experience in Rhodesia earlier. Thus, these machines were available for hasty conversion and, from July 1960 onwards, they served in the COIN role during the war of Independence in the Belgian Congo.

After independence had been granted the bulk of the training aircraft were written-off and scrapped when the Belgian Air Force pulled out but six of the Harvards subsequently served with the Air Force of Ruanda-Urundi. From 1960 to 1962 they fought again during their own Congolese Civil War.

The Royal Danish Air Force obtained twenty-seven Mark IIB Harvards from the RAF from December 1946 to September 1947, plus four more from Canada. From South Africa via the UK a further seven were received for spares.

The Royal Norwegian Air Force received twenty-three Harvard Mark IIBs from the former Norwegian Training Base at Winkleigh on its closure in November 1945. Seven further ex-Canadian Harvards joined them later.

The Royal Swedish Air Force as related equipped itself with 144 ex-Canadian Mark IIBs (as the SK-16). They also bought former SNJ-2, -3 and -4s from surplus stocks post-war. A total of 257 aircraft were purchased in this manner. These all served with the F5 Primary Training School at Ljungbyhed through to 1968. One of these trainers survived, Fv16109 (formerly FE 632) and is now preserved at the Swedish Air Force Museum at Linkoping.

The *Fliegerabwehrtruppen* (Swiss Air Force) purchased forty Noorduyn-built Harvard IIBs from the RCAF in 1947 and these were given the Swiss Serials U-301 to U-340. On their arrival in Europe they were given a complete overhaul by the Dutch firms of Aviolanda and Fokker of Amsterdam and Schipol. From 1949 to 1968 they served with great success as blind-flying instruction machines, for, in this period, practically all military trainee pilots obtained the blind-flying qualification. They were employed strictly as training and liaison aircraft and no armament was *ever* carried.

When the new Pilatus P3-03/05 training aircraft arrived, blind-flying instruction was commenced in the flying schools, so that the AT-6 was less and less required. Furthermore, by 1968, they were well overdue for a major overhaul of airframe parts suffering from fatigue. The whole AT-6 fleet was therefore withdrawn from service and scrapped, except two aircraft and four engines which were retained as exhibits.

Aircraft number U-322 was bought by an English institition. It received the civil registration G-AXCR and was flown from Dubendorf to London via Kloten and Cologne on 10 April 1969. With the exception of those retained for exhibits, all engines, plus propellers and engine mounting units, were purchased by an American aircraft maintenance company and delivered to Dallas, Texas for use in twin-engined ground-spraying aircraft.

The Royal Hellenic Air Force obtained thirty-five Harvard Mk IIAs from South Africa via Britain between March and August 1947 and thirty Mark IIBs direct from the UK from July 1947 onwards.

The Turkish Air Force received a grand total of 196 T-6/Harvard aircraft. The first batch of one hundred machines, AT-6Cs, arrived in the country on 2 August 1948 and were given Turkish Serials 7251 to 7350. These were later supplemented by eighteen ex-RAF Harvard Mark IIBs from the Royal Norwegian Air Force, six arriving on 4 October 1955 and twelve more on 6 November 1955. They received the Turkish Serials 7351 to 7368. These were followed, on 18 July 1956, by a further eight Mark II Harvards that arrived from RCAF sources and were numbered 7369 to 7376.

Under the NATO Mutual Air Programme Turkey received yet further batches of North American COIN and trainer aircraft. The first of these new assignments were sixteen former LT-6Gs. These arrived on 7 September 1957 and were assigned Serial Numbers 7377 to 7392. They were followed by three more of the same type on 7 October 1957 (7393 to 7395) along with eleven T-6Gs (7396 to 7399 and 7501 to 7505).

Two more consignments were shipped to Turkey in 1958. On 13 January of that year twenty-one machines arrived and were numbered 7508 to 7528), while on 5 May 1958 a final batch of nineteen were received (7529 to 7547).

All these aircraft served on the Turkish Air Force Inventory for over twenty-five years, the final T-6 being phased out in 1976.

The Yugoslavian Air Force obtained ten Harvard Mark IIBs, direct from the UK to use at the local Flying Training School, which was then operating as part of the Allied Mediterranean Air Force, in March and April 1945. Post-war, the Communist Government emulated their Russian mentors and held on to their 'loaned' aircraft after the war had terminated.

In the Middle-East the former Royal Iranian Air Force had armed T-6Gs on its strength prior to the overthrow of the Shah, which it used against Kurdish insurgents.

Harvards served with the Israeli Defence Force and Air Force during the 1948 War of Independence where they fought armed as dive-bombers with two .50 calibre machine-guns in the wings and a .30 gun on a flexible mounting aft. They were also adapted to carry eight 110-lb bombs on underwing racks or alternatively 400lb of bombs.

Again in 1956 rocket-firing and bombing Israeli T-6s fought against Egyptian armoured forces. However, they suffered severe damage from the sophisticated Egyptian anti-aircraft defences and were not combat employed again. They were pensioned off from training duties in 1965.

There were twenty Syrian Air Force armed Harvards T-6s. Ten of these were ex-RAF Mark IIBs from South African stocks in 1956.

Three Harvard Mark IIBs from the RAF's 1340 Flight in Kenya were re-supplied to the Royal Jordanian Air Force in January and February 1956.

The Lebanese Air Force obtained sixteen Harvards which it obtained from various British sources between 1952 and 1954.

In Africa the Mozambique Government inherited some former Portuguese Air Force Harvards after Independence. These were soon withdrawn from flying duties and were parked in open storage at Maputo Airport, where they remained exposed to the elements and steadily deteriorated.

Biafran insurgent forces, using mercenary pilots, flew twelve ex-French T-6s against Nigerian forces during their struggle for independence between 1967-1970 and are credited with destroying one Nigerian Air Force MiG-17 'Fresco' jet fighter on the ground in that conflict.

South Africa has long been the major user of the Harvard. Indeed it owns the largest Harvard air fleet in the world. Several score remain of the hundreds she inherited from the war and remain on her training school inventory today. She was also a major user of the type in the ground-attack role particularly against SWAPO guerrilla forces in South-West Africa (Namibia) and against Mozambique incursions across her frontiers.

Although the RAF continued to fly Harvard aircraft from Negombo (now Katunayake) airfield right up to 1952, none were taken into service when Ceylon became independent Sri Lanka.

The Indian Air Force Harvards initially saw much hard *combat* duty during the Kashmir Operation, which commenced on 28 October 1947. Pakistan and India fought over this disputed territory and ground-strafing became a priority. Two days later two IAF Harvards, which had been hastily adapted to the close support role at Ambala, were rushed forward to work from Srinagar airfield. On 31 October these Harvards gave air support to the infantry and two further machines were sent to join them. Aviation fuel had to be flown into the advance airfield by Dakotas, transferred to buckets and poured in the Harvards' fuel tanks to keep the missions going. On 4 November 1947 the Harvards again sortied over the battlefield in the Badgam-Baramulla Sector to good effect.

Reconnaissance missions were flown over Kotli by the Harvards on 3 November and they also attacked Pakistan fortified positions. Another valuable contribution the IAF Harvards from Srinagar gave the Army was rendered on 5 November when four machines were sent out to first locate, and then guide an Indian armoured column from the Banihal Pass to Srinagar, which it did in the following two days. This enabled the major Indian ground attack to be put in on the 7th.

When the Indian advance was held up near Rampur on 12 November, two Harvards joined in the close-support missions and attacked Domel, Kotli, Mirpur and Uri, and the latter town fell next day. On 16 November close-support was given to Indian troops at Uri and enemy positions around a road block at Milepost 67 were bombed, strafed and destroyed by them.

Back in the more tranquil training role the Harvards continued to give their usual sterling service. Late in 1963 the Indian Air Force Harvards were concentrated soley at the AFFC. Ten years later the Harvard was still being used, alongside the new Indian-designed and built HJT-16 Kiran jet trainer, with the AFA. Not until 1975 was the last Harvard phased out of service on the sub-continent, after more than thirty years faithful flying.

In September 1946, the Royal New Zealand Air Force formerly absorbed the survivors of all her wartime deliveries, plus acquiring one Mark IIB in 1948. They served until 24 June 1977. One still survives, NZ1015 (formerly the RAF EX193) and is part of the RNZAF Historic Flight.

The Japanese Self Defense Force took delivery of both T-6Fs and SNJ-6s early in October 1957 and used them until 1976. Japan became the fourth nation to build the type under licence (after Sweden, Australia and Canada).

The Laotian Air Force T-6s flew missions against the Communist Pathet Lao guerrillas and along the Ho Chi Minh Trail during the Vietnam War.

The Royal Thai Air Force obtained T-6s direct from the States between 1948 and 1957. They operated with 1, 2, 3, 4, 5, 6 and 7 Wings and they formed three Attack Groups with them. The T-6s served as well as the RTAF Flying Training School at Don Muang, Bangkok, until 1974.

The Chinese Nationalist Air Force in Formosa also acquired a number of T-6s. Likewise the Philippine Air Force was the recipient of many T-6Gs.

In South America, Brazil used armed T-6s, fitted with underwing racks for rockets and light bombs in the COIN role. T-6GS also served with the Liaison and Observation Squadrons of the Brazilian Air Force in this configuration and were equipped with a life-raft carried in an under-the-fuselage container. The premier Brazilian formation team to use the Harvard was the *Esquadrilla de Fumaca* (Smoke-trailing Squadron). They gave numerous displays in their T-6s, which were strikingly painted with red wing-tips, black underbellies and a horizontal red lightning flash down the white fuselage. They served in this duty from 1956 until 7 February 1963 when the T-6s were replaced by FAB T-24 jet trainers.

The Chilean, Mexican, Uruguayan and Venezuelan Air Forces were among many Latin American air fleets equipped with AT-6Ds post-war. Some South American nations still fly the odd T-6 in the COIN role today.

In the last two decades, however, it is as a civilian pleasure machine that the Texan has spent its most productive years. A whole variety of roles have presented themselves to the North American, and I have tried to include as many representatives as possible in these pages to cover these, from stunt machine to racer to rebuilt show machine.

In the latter configuration, in 1989, the Oshkosh Grand Champion was a Harvard Mark IV (20247). This aircraft contained almost all its original authentic parts rather than being built from new ones. This model was a Canadian Car and Foundry produced aircraft, the final one of the series, built in 1955. It was based at Penhold, Alberta with 4 Fighter Trainer Squadron, RCAF, and logged 4,191 hours of flying time. After an accident in 1958 it was repaired and overhauled with new right elevator, wing flaps, centre section, vertical stabilizer, starboard wing and hydraulic assemblies. It then soldiered on at Penhold until 1964, totalling 6,512 flying hours and six engine changes. On retirement its wings were removed, engine and propeller moth-balled and the aircraft placed in storage. It was finally struck from charge on 28 February 1966.

The Harvard was ferried to Chino, California and remained stored until 1988 when Bill Melamed of Los Angeles bought her to restore her. The work was done by John Muszala of Pacific Fighters using as many of the original parts as possible. The engine was overhauled and inspection showed the original fabric of the control surfaces in perfect condition. The original radio was made to work, but the addition of modern equipment was deemed necessary for safety, but it is mounted on a removable panel. By the time the aircraft was complete it was more than ninety-seven per cent original. Painted yellow, with day-glo pink cowling and rudder, Bill's Harvard was the deserving winner after all this careful work.

Long may the 'Noisy North American' continue to grace the skies of the world.

(*previous page*)

The T-6 and its many variants are now the most popular of the propeller driven vintage civilian aircraft still flying today. Their popularity has undergone troughs and peaks since that time, because keeping them flying costs a lot of money and time. In 1952 just over three hundred remained on the register, but, in reverse ratio to the machines' age, this figure began to rise once more, helped by the retirement of numerous machines from the military services, to over four hundred two decades later.

Here Jim Larsen's immaculate camera work catches an equally immaculate 'JAX' over the Sierras in the late 1970s. (*Jim Larsen Photographs, Kirkland, Washington*)

Whole societies have grown up, again especially in the States, built around the Texan. The more recent 'Warbird' scene is one of the more interesting innovations. Here T-6s and Harvards have again featured strongly (if not always very accurately) in the re-creation of wartime aircraft in flyable form down to passing imitations flown for fun and spectacle, with no pretence at 'exactness' of colour scheme or markings. NA-16s and their successors are classified as officially 'Classic' aircraft by the Experimental Aircraft Association in its Antiques and Classics Division. The Sport Aviation Association section of this organisation has offices at Franklin, Wisconsin and a European branch at Welwyn Garden City, just north of London.

Here a Mark IV Harvard, (AJ832 BH-S) is seen with wheels down coming in for a landing and carrying an RAF dazzle paint scheme complete with duck-egg blue band around fuselage, yellow wing-tips, propeller extremities and edging to the old-type roundels. (*Jim Larsen Photographs, Kirkland, Washington*)

'GOTCHA!' Making a stunning contrast between the sparkling Pacific ocean and the gleaming scarlet of her paintwork this T-6G is one of many restored to their former glory and fully flightworthy after dedicated work by T-6 enthusiasts in the States.

The North American Trainer Association is another really flourishing organisation and, under the Presidentship of Stoney Stonich, has almost four-hundred pilot members in the States. The T-6 Owners Association flourishes and in conjunction with the Warbirds of America encourage the maintenance, promotion and safety aspects of T-6 restoration, flying and exhibition. There is also an equally active and wide-ranging 'Mosquito' Association for LT-6G veterans of the Korean conflict. (*Jim Larsen Photographs, Kirkland, Washington*)

A splendid airborne view of *How Sweet It Is* from the Swayze team of Mesquite, Texas, who regularly sweep the board at Oshkosh with their immaculate paintwork and meticulously assembled flying T-6s. This glittering all-metal finish beauty was his first effort and well worth every loving hour of care spent on her. (*Courtesy 'Doc' Swayze, Mesquite, Texas*)

Another 'Doc' Swayze re-build, one of six T-6s he and his team have lovingly built and flown down the years. This is the latest, an SNJ-5 (N5486V) which carries the pre-World War II paint scheme of the US aircraft carrier *Saratoga* with red tail and cowling and yellow wings.

Totally built from new surplus parts and completed in June 1987, 5486V won for the Swayze team their third National Award for the Best AT-6 at Oshkosh in 1987. (*Courtesy 'Doc' Swayze, Mesquite, Texas*)

Air Racing has been another aspect of aviation interest to strongly feature the T-6 in all its many aspects. Pylon and Long-Distance meetings always feature several of the type at any assembly. When the National Air Races at Cleveland resumed, the prestigious female event, the Halle Trophy Race, was dominated by T-6s with cockpits removed and engines supercharged for those vital extra knots. It was won that year by Ruth Johnson flying a highly 'souped-up' AT-6, in which she achieved a speed of over 223 mph, after the X-Birds had both dropped out as related earlier. Second place was taken by Grace Harris. In 1948 this event became the Kendall Trophy race and Grace Harris won it in that year, and the next, by which time supercharged engines and three-bladed propellers had been banned from the competition.

Again, there was a two-decade lull in the sport but, in 1967, the T-6 re-appeared at the National Air Races now held at Reno, Nevada. This set the ball in motion once more and the following year there were seventeen entries for the Bardahl Trophy race for standard T-6s, and so it has continued to this day.

Here an early T-Bird flyer (N7067C) is shown at Monterey, California, airstrip in July 1968. (*Courtesy Nick Williams Collection*)

(above)
Gary Numan inverted! Since joining the Harvard Formation Team the pop star and showman has enthusiastically embraced the Harvard flying technique and lent his own brand of uniqueness to their flying displays and aerobatics! The team travel all over the world giving their displays and between May and October of most years are fully committed in the United Kingdom as well. Although the former RAF fighter base located close to Harlow New Town has had a slice of its runway cut off by the M11 motorway, it is still more than adequate to house the team and the Annual 'Warbirds Fighter Meet' takes place there as well.

The Harvard Team is sponsored by Tarmac Construction of Milton Keynes and each year at the famous Cranfield Air Races and Air Show, held annually at the Bedfordshire airfield, there is a special 'Harvard Trophy' to be competed for on an individual basis. (*Courtesy of The Squadron, Harvard Formation Team, North Weald*)

(below)
Two T-6s drop down on the dusty airstrip at Mojave, California, in October 1974, while in the distance, another brace circle in readiness to follow them down. 'Air Meets' of this kind have increased the popularity of the T-6 family with civilian owners the world over.

Flyable aircraft are always more exciting than static display models of course, although, usually, the latter are much more likely to be both authentic machines and well documented. However, there are exceptions! In South Korea, for example, the Korean War Museum in Seoul has a static ROKAF T-6 on display. In 1989 Captain Russ Turner, USAF, reported on this aircraft. 'Although weathered, it's complete. It has two machine-gun pods and four bomb racks. The display states that the initial invasion from the north was met by South Korean T-6s pelting the communists with grenades!' Just what the Mosquito veterans think of that claim is uncertain!

In Australia and New Zealand both Harvard and Wirraway have been enjoying similar popularity and only a shortage of suitable aircraft has prevented a similar expansion to that found in the UK and the USA. (*Courtesy Nick Williams Collection*)

(*above*)
This SNJ is seen landing at the Hawthorne Air Fair in 1987. Painted brilliant red it has the markings 'China Lake' on its tail. China Lake, California, is a Naval Weapons Test Station but this is probably just a restoration by enthusiasts there, although very well done.

The fiftieth anniversary of the North American Texan type was marked in 1988 by a number of special celebrations around the world. In the States the North American Trainer Association marked the event at Kenosha, Wisconsin, between 23 and 27 July when almost 150 T-6s and derivatives flew in what was the largest gathering of the type in one place since the US military discontinued the type in service.

As things look today the planning for the 60th, and even the 70th anniversary of this remarkable aircraft can be started with confidence. The resilience of the T-6 marks it out as one of the most outstanding aircraft of all time. Long may she continue to grace our skies! (*Courtesy Dr Ira Chart*)

(*overleaf*)
It was the relative simplicity of the T-6 that enamoured it of civilian owners, especially in the USA. In November 1945 only small modifications were needed to bring the AT-6/SNJs into line to meet Government guidelines. This allowed them to gain the required Commercial Civil Aircraft licence 'ticket' for revenue operating, (although it was only the Category 2-575 certificate). It did not prove possible for the former military Texans to gain the full Approved Type certificate (ATC) in the States. It was Autair, a London company, that later received the more limiting AR-11 'Restricted' ticket for the AT-16s. In this way more than eight-hundred former T-6 variants were on the civilian register by 1947, working in a wide variety of roles.

This appeal is world-wide and this privately-owned and exotically painted T-6H was proudly on display at a 'Fly-In' in West Germany in 1988. (*Courtesy Hanfried Schliephake Archive*)

153

Appendix 1: T-6 Namecheck:

Throughout its long career the North American trainer has received a whole variety of names quite apart from the many company and official designations. Depending on how pendantic the reader is (or how much of a 'nit-picker') the blood pressure of enthusiasts rises in proportion to the number of times the 'wrong' word is used. In this volume, as a very general rule of thumb, the name 'T-6' has been used as the overall covering name for *all* the variants. Beneath this blanket, in order to prevent too much repetition, the name 'AT-6' has been used for older models and 'T-6' for all post T-6Gs. Appendix 2 covers the company and official designations.

For the rest, the following list gives a quick summary check on the various official and unofficial titles received by the aircraft described in this book, with a brief word on the probably origins.

BACON SUPER: an American one-off civilian conversion of a standard T-6 into a counter-insurgency/ground-attack aircraft.

BOOMERANG: the CAC-designed and built WW II Australian fighter aircraft built utilising some Wirraway parts and fixtures.

C.6: the Spanish post-war ground-attack conversions.

CERES: not a conversion but a CAC Australian-built and designed post-war crop-spraying aircraft.

HARVARD: the British and Commonwealth name given to American and Canadian-built variants of the T-6. Four different Marks.

HURRICANE HUNTER: not strictly the name of the aircraft themselves but their unit, the American All-Weather patrols, but sometimes applied to the aircraft themselves.

J-BIRD: the popular US Navy term for the SNJ variants.

LEMON BOMBER: derisive West German Luftwaffe term for post-war T-6 trainers derived from their colouring.

MOSQUITO: the radio call-sign of the American LT-6G close-support aircraft in the Korean War which was adopted for both the aircraft and the unit itself.

NOISY NORTH AMERICAN: a wry British term used mainly by ground staff and aircrew in the UK, for obvious reasons.

OAK: the Allied WW II codename allocated to the Japanese training derivative, the Kyushu K10W.

RANGER: general term for the Ranger-engined XAT and its post-war copy.

SK-16: the Royal Swedish Air Force licence-built variant of the T-6.

TEXAN: the 'Official' name given to Dallas-built AT-6s said to have originated from both the plant and the numerous Texas-based flying schools. Later applied to all AT-6 and T-6s, but *not* generally adopted by the American aircrews themselves during the war.

TOMCAT: the French Air Forces' name for their ground-attack conversions during the Algerian war.

WIRRAWAY: the WW II CAC Australian licence-built trainer/dive-bomber variant of the AT-6.

YALE: British and Commonwealth name allocated to the American-built fixed-under-carriage predecessor of the AT-6.

Appendix 2:
NAA Variant Listing:

On 27 May 1956, North American Aviation issued Report 'O' from which a breakdown of the company Charge Numbers and designations, along with quantities and serial numbers of all the trainers of the series could be listed. This enabled the company Charge Number (NA-) to be checked against the Model designation (AT-). An original (more detailed) compilation was done by historian Dustin W. Carter many years ago, to whose dedication and application I am accordingly deeply indebted.

This listing serves two functions. Firstly, it enables the direct lineal descent of the T-6 to be followed in a chronological sequence. Secondly, it assists further research. As both the original company drawings and many major sub-assemblies are solely identified by the NA-numbers, this cross-over reference is important for archive checking. It is also important for the reader to understand that *only* machines actually constructed or modified by NAA are included in this list. For private conversions, Canadian, Australian and other licence-built variants, along with USAAF, USAF and USN modifications are *not* included here.

CHARGE No.	DATE	DESIGNATION	CUSTOMER	QUANTITY	FACTORY S/N
NA-16	–	NA-16	–	1	NA-16-1
NA-18	13-5-35	NA-18	Argentina	–	NA-18-1
NA-19	10-3-35	BT-9	USAAC	42	NA-19-1 NA-19-3 NA-19-5/11 NA-19-20/34 NA-19-50/67
NA-19A	–	BT-9A	USAAC Reserve	40	NA-19-4 NA-19-12/19 NA-19-35/49 NA-19-68/83
NA-20	–	NA-16-2H	Honduras	1	NA-16-2
NA-22	–	NA-22	USAAC	–	NA-16-1
NA-23	1-12-36	BT-9B	USAAC	117	NA-23-85/201
NA-26	20-10-36	BC-1	Canada	1	26-202
NA-27	1-12-36	NA-16-2H	Fokker	1	27-312
NA-28	14-12-36	NJ-1	USAAC for USN	40	28-313/352
NA-29	22-12-36	BT-9C	USAAC Reserve	32	29-353/384
		YIBT-10	USAAC	1	29-385
		BT-9C	USAAC	34	29-505/538
NA-30	–	YIBT-10	–	–	–
NA-31	2-8-37	NA 16-4M	Sweden	1	31-386

NA-32	10-3-37	NA-16-1-A	Australia for CAC	1	32-387
NA-33	10-3-37	NA-16-2K	Australia for CAC	1	33-388
NA-34	19-3-37	NA-16-4P	Argentina	30	34-389/418
NA-36	16-6-37	BC-1	USAAC	85 92	36-420/504 36-596/687
NA-37	2-9-37	NA-16-4R	Japan	1	37-539
NA-38	28-9-37	NA-16-4M	Sweden	1	38-540
NA-41	23-2-38	NA-16-4	China	35	41-697/731
NA-42	9-12-37	NA-16-2A	Honduras	2	42-691/692
NA-43	9-12-37	NA-16-1Q	Brazil	–	Cancelled
NA-44	9-12-37	NA-44	Canada	1	44-747
NA-45	14-12-37	NA-16-IGV	Venezuela	3	45-693/695
NA-46	2-12-38	NA-16-4	Brazil	12	46-972/977 46-1991/1996
NA-47	16-12-37	NA-16-4RW	Japan	1	47-699
NA-48	23-2-38	NA-16-3C	China	15	48-732/746
NA-49	7-2-38	NA-16-IE Harvard I	UK	200 200	49-748/947 49-1053/1252
NA-50	9-2-39	NA-50	Peru	7	50-948/954
NA-52	28-9-38	SNJ-1	USN	16	52-956/971
NA-54	3-10-38	BC-2	USAAC	3	54-688/690
NA-55	–	BC-1A	USAAC	83	55-1548/1630
NA-56	18-4-39	NA-16-4	China	50	56-1453/1502
NA-57	21-2-39	NA-57 (BT-9B)	France	230	57-1253/1452 57-1518/1547
NA-58	28-4-39	BT-14	USAAC	251	58-1655/1905
NA-59	–	AT-6	USAAC	94	59-1631/1639 59-1906/1990
NA-61	25-5-39	NA-16-IE	Canada	30	61-1503/1517 61-1640/1654
NA-64	5-9-39	NA-64	France	230	64-2033/2232 64-3018/3047
NA-65	25-9-39	SNJ-2	USN	36	65-1997/2032
NA-66	17-11-39	Harvard II	UK	600	66-2234/2833

NA-68	30-11-39	NA-50A (P-64)	Siam	6	68-3058/3063
NA-69	30-11-39	NA-44	Siam	10	60-3064-3073
NA70	9-1-40	Cancelled	–	–	–
NA-71	18-1-40	NA-16-3	Venezuela	3	71-3074/3076
NA-72	13-1-40	NA-44 (BC-1A)	Brazil	30	72-3077/3096 72-4757/4766
NA-74	7-8-40	NA-44	Chile	12	74-4745/4756
NA-75	3-6-40	Harvard II	Canada	100	75-3048/3057 75-3418/3507
NA-76	5-6-40	Harvard II	UK	450	76-3508/3957
NA-77	28-6-40	AT-6A SNJ-3	USAAC	517 120	–
NA-78	1-10-40	AT-6A SNJ-3	USAAC USN	1330 150	–
NA-79	–	SNJ-2	USN	25	78-3983/4007
NA-81	11-7-40	Harvard II	UK	125	81-4008/4132
NA-84	6-12-40	AT-6B	USAAC	400	78-7412/7811
NA-85	–	SNJ-3	–	–	To NA-78
NA-88	10-4-41 –	AT-6C AT-6D SNJ-4 SNJ-5	USAAF USAAF USN USN	2970 2604 2400 1357	
NA-119	10-1-44	AT-6D	USAAF (for Brazil)	81	119-40086/40166
NA-121	11-2-44	AT-6D AT-6F	USAAF	800 956	121-41567/42366 121-42367/43322
NA-128	1-6-44	Cancelled	–	–	–
NA-168	5-10-49	T-6G	USAF	641	168-1/371 168-387/440 168-450/500 168-511/560 168-571/620 168-631/680 168-681/691
		LT-6G T-6G	USAF ANG	59 50	168-692/750 168-372/381 168-441/450 168-501/510 168-561/570 168-621/630
NA-182	8-2-51	T-6G	USAF	824	182-1/824

NA-186	22-6-51	T-6J	USAF	–	Design data
NA-188	11-4-51	T-6G	USAF	100 7	188-1/100 188-101/107
NA-195	19-3-52	T-6G	USAF	11	191-1/11
NA-197 FO.8002	16-6-52	T-6G	USAF (T-6D to T-6G for ANG)	50 60	197-1/50 8002-1/60
NA-198	Terminated 3-7-52		USN	240	–

For acrobatic display and formation flying, few aircraft can beat the North American trainer. The combined racket of six or more P&Ws snarling overhead is usually worth the admission money alone! Instant reaction had long been a hall-mark of the North American trainer and superb wing-tip to wing-tip displays are grist to its mill. During the war inverted flight time was limited to ten seconds due to the dry-sump oil condition but the machine is light on the controls.

In Great Britain the premier team is 'The Harvard Formation Team' based at the former Battle of Britain airfield of North Weald, near Harlow, Essex. Here 087 of that team bids a fond farewell to Oshkosh! (*Courtesy of The Squadron, Harvard Formation Team, North Weald*)

Sky-writing and publicity banner-hauling has also naturally featured on the working T-6's itinerary down the years. In the mid-1960s a new slant on that old advertising ploy is used by the American firm of Skytypers East, based at Flushing, New York. Six former SNJ-2s are used in a technique known as 'Skytyping'. Linked together electronically, a 'master' lead plane acts as guide and controller with a main computer and transmitter aboard. On the word from this machine all six aircraft, known as the Miller Squadron after the Brewery firm which sponsors them, simultaneously 'type' out a letter by emitting smoke balls at about 1,000ft altitude. Seen from the ground this merges into readily readable writing at the rate of nine characters per minute. This is a ten-fold improvement on the old-style skywriting and has proved a big hit. Each 'letter' extends over about five miles of airspace and is highly effective.

The line-up of the Skytyping T-6s (with N66082 in the foreground) is seen here at Long Beach, California, in July 1968, where a West Coast team was set up. (*Courtesy N.M. Williams Collection*)